Our Village School:
The Saga of the Stove

Summer 2020

To Hayley,

Thank you for all your hard work.
Here is something to look back on
when you think of Castleton!

All the best
from

the pupils, parents + staff
of Castleton.

Our Village School: The Saga of the Stove

THE HISTORY OF CASTLETON COMMUNITY PRIMARY SCHOOL, NORTH YORKSHIRE

1874 - 2014

BY
CAROL M. WILSON

First published by the North Yorkshire Moors Association, 2014

© 2014 Carol Wilson

A copy of the British Library Cataloguing in Publication Data
is available from the British Library

ISBN 978-0-9565779-3-1

Front cover photograph – from a postcard by T. Watson of Lythe *circa* 1910.
Back cover photograph – school in the snow 1990s.

Designed and typeset by Basement Press, Glaisdale (www.basementpress.com)
Printed and bound by Inprint Colour, Malton

All proceeds from the sale of this book to Castleton School Fund.

The Ainthorpe Educational Trust is a local charitable foundation that funds pupils in the parishes of Danby and Westerdale. Parents and pupils are invited to apply to the trust for money towards educational projects such as school trips or equipment. The trust meets at the beginning of each term to allocate funds. For further information please contact the school.

For further information about the school go to: www.castleton.n-yorks.sch.uk

CASTLETON SCHOOL MISSION STATEMENT

Together we aim to encourage the development of
lively enquiring minds, independence and self discipline
and to foster a rightful sense of self worth and responsibility,
which will encourage perseverance
and which will lead to personal fulfilment.

Contents

	Foreword	ix
	Preface	x
Chapter 1	The Early Years	1
Chapter 2	The Headship of Mr Groves	13
Chapter 3	Between the Wars and Immediate Post-War Years	19
Chapter 4	The 1950s, 60s and 70s	31
Chapter 5	The 1980s and 1990s	45
Chapter 6	The New Millennium	63
	Afterword	89
Appendix 1	Head teachers at Castleton School 1874 – 2014	90
Appendix 2	Number on Roll	91
Appendix 3	Standards of Education from the Revised Code of Regulations, 1872	92
Appendix 4	Money, Weights and Measures	94
Appendix 5	Children at Castleton School in the Centenary Year 1974	95
Appendix 6	Children at the School at the 140th Anniversary, November 2014	96
Appendix 7	Staff and Governors of Castleton Community Primary School 2014	97

This book is dedicated to all of the pupils, staff, managers and governors of Castleton School past, present and future

Foreword

$\mathcal{A}$FTER THE PASSING of the 1867 Reform Act, the then Chancellor of the Exchequer, Robert Lowe, remarked that the government would now 'have to educate our masters'. Subsequently the government passed the 1870 Education Act, which set the framework for schooling of all children between the ages of 5 and 13. Most villages were then to have their own elementary school.

Built on land that was given by the Dawnay family, the school at Castleton was opened in 1874 with an initial intake of 65. The early records show that the children were repeatedly absent and parents complained about children being caned or having to sweep the classroom after lessons. How very different schooling was in those days!

Compiled from the school's log books, *Our Village School* is a fascinating account of the history of Castleton School – and you will soon discover why it is subtitled *the Saga of the Stove*. Written to celebrate the school's 140th anniversary it reads like a social history and also contains some interesting early photographs.

Lady Downe
Wykeham 2014

Preface

IN APRIL 2000 I was appointed as head teacher at Castleton Community Primary School in North Yorkshire. I was to take up my post from September of that year. For me this was a childhood dream come true; I was to lead my own village school.

From the outset I thought that I would like to write the history of the school. While Castleton School, like any school, has its particular style and story to tell there are aspects of a Victorian school that are common to all and that tell part of our country's social history. One of the first things that I did was to read through the log books to see how the school had got to its present position. Later I was to read them through at least three more times and I have done so again recently. Headship, however, took up most of my time and then retirement led to more studying for myself. This year, as the school approaches its 140th anniversary, seemed to be the ideal time to write the story of *Our Village School*.

This is not the story of any single child's years through the school, nor is it about every member of staff who has worked here over the years. It is about the development of the school and what has gone on here over 140 years. Inevitably, I have had to leave out a great deal more of the story than I have been able to include; I hope that readers will not be too disappointed if their favourite story has not been printed. I have tried to pick out major developments over the years, especially the changes to the fabric of the school. I have also tried to include items and issues from every decade and the important changes made by each head teacher over the years.

None of this would have been possible without the help and co-operation of many people. First of all I would like to thank each and every member of staff who helped me to run the school during my time in headship. I had a wonderful team – governors, teaching staff, classroom assistants, kitchen staff, a very practical cleaner-cum-caretaker as well as a first class school secretary – all of whom gave above and beyond the call of duty. Thank you to the present head teacher, Jane Douglass, for making me so welcome in the school and for making the log books available to me. Mrs Douglass is also to be thanked for contributions to the last chapter and for proof reading that section of the book.

Many thanks go to Jacqueline Chapman for allowing the use of the photograph of Dora Duck as well as her nineteenth-century exercise books, to Emma Beeforth and Emma Skidmore for the use of the early photographs of the school and to Alan Meek for looking in the attic. I am particularly grateful to Emma Beeforth for allowing the inclusion of photographs of her mother's school needlework. Thanks to Emma and to Betty Medd (both now in their nineties) for remembering the names of so many of the children on photographs from the 1920s.

Slide photographs from the 1970s were taken by the late Miss Loo; thank you to Michael Wilson for digitising these for printing. Many thanks to Dave Chapman for his contribution about the years when he was head of the school, and for proof reading Chapter 5, and to Connie Watson for her memories and the loan of her photographs from her years as infant teacher. Thank you to Elaine Keogh for the use of her centenary programme and to Marna Pacey for the loan of photographs. Thank you to Sue Playle-Watson for the photograph of the garden opening and for Louis for being such a good sport. Thank you to Anne King for taking the photograph of former staff. A special thank you goes to Lewis Hughes for photographs, including those from *Bugsy Malone* and who was also able to identify the children in the football and netball teams (with a little help from Steph Raw). Thank you to all of those who have helped to identify individuals in other photographs. Some of the photographs have been difficult to date so their captions read *circa*, meaning about, but if anyone is able to date any of them more accurately I would be pleased to know.

Thank you to Pam Shepherd for the use of her album and scrapbook records of the years when she was at the school and thanks to Pam and to Delia Liddle, Albert Elliot and Elizabeth Cruickshank for proof reading, although any remaining errors are my own.

I am grateful to Summerdale Publishers Ltd for giving permission for the use of images from the Janet and John reading books *Here We Go* and *Off to Play*. Thank you to Tempest Photography for permission to reproduce school photographs. Thank you to Duncan Atkins of the *Whitby Gazette* for searching the *Gazette*'s archives of photographs and for permission to use those included in the book. And special thanks to Beamish Museum for allowing me to photograph Victorian School artefacts, including the school stove, from their collection and for their support for this project.

Thank you to the Westerdale History Group, the David Ross Foundation, Danby Health Shop and to all those who have supported local money-raising events for funding towards the printing and publication costs of the book. Special thanks are due to Nicola Chalton and Pascal Thivillon of Basement Press, Glaisdale, who have arranged the typesetting and made the book fit for publication, especially the treatment of some faded old photographs; they have done a wonderful job. Likewise the printers, Inprint Colour, who have made such a splendid final copy, and to the North Yorkshire Moors Association who agreed to publish the book. Last but by no means least I must say a very special thank you to my husband, Nigel, whom I met while I was in headship at Castleton. At Pam Shepherd's suggestion he created the graph of pupil numbers for Appendix 2. He has seen me through thick and thin over a number of projects, not least this one. To all, my heart-felt gratitude.

For readers' interest I have included a list of all of the head teachers at the school as well as the numbers of children on roll, for the years where the numbers were readily available. You will also find appended the nineteenth-century Standards within schools and an explanation of current year groups. This is followed by a list of the children in the school in 1974, the centenary year. I have also included lists of all those at Castleton in 2014, as the school celebrates its 140th anniversary.

As an additional note, in view of the pre-metric information included in this book, it should be remembered that in those faraway days there were four farthings or two halfpennies to the penny, 12 pence to the shilling and 20 shillings to the pound (£ s. d.; the d stood for *denarius*, the Latin word for a penny). Two shillings and sixpence made half a crown and £1 1s equalled one guinea. There were 16 ounces (oz) to the pound (lb) weight, 14 pounds to the stone and 8 stones or 112 pounds to the hundredweight (cwt). There were 12 inches to the foot and 3 feet to the yard. Longer lengths were measured in rods, poles and perches, furlongs and chains while 4,840 square yards made an acre. These measurements of length date back to Anglo Saxon times and are based on plough land measures. Volume was measured in pints and gallons. The Winchester measure, which established a standard measurement of volume, was introduced by Henry VII in the late fifteenth century. Together these measurements are known as the imperial system of weights and measures.

All of this made learning tables an essential part of school life and those of us of mature years can still remember the morning chant of 16 ounces one pound, 14 pounds one stone as well as 12 pence one shilling, 20 pence one and 8 pence, 24 pence two shillings, etc. It made for some interesting arithmetic gymnastics. Tables of imperial weights and measures and those of the former monetary system are also included at the end of the book.

Carol Wilson
Westerdale 2014

The Early Years

CASTLETON SCHOOL started life as Castleton Board School. It was sometimes referred to as Danby Board School and DBS is carved onto the right-hand stone gatepost of the smaller gate. Built on land given by Lord Downe, it was opened by the head master, Mr William Bull, on November 16th 1874, duly recorded in the first school log book (Fig 1.1). The school opened with 65 pupils aged five to eleven. By the following January the average attendance was 103, all taught together in one large classroom. It must have been very crowded indeed.

Mr Bull's early comments do not seem to take account of the fact that most of the children would not have been to school before. Many of his early entries into the log book are in fact more to do with practical issues than they are to do with education. He was especially concerned about heating and lighting and having the classroom swept at the end of each school day.

> January 4th 1875 *School very dark and classroom full of smoke. Boys, two each week, were appointed to sweep the school by order of the Board.*[1]

By February one parent was refusing to allow his son to sweep the school and by the following November the head master was complaining that four boys had neglected to sweep the school and that it was difficult to get the job done properly. He continued to record poor light levels but at least they had got the stoves working...for a time.

Fig. 1.1 The first page of the first log book of Castleton School.

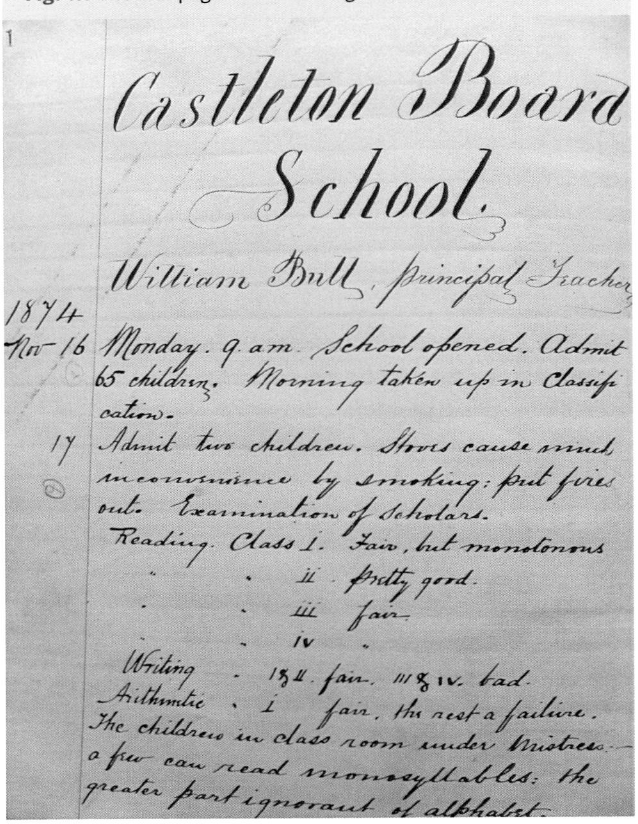

Castleton Board School.

William Bull, principal Teacher

1874

Nov 16 Monday. 9 am. School opened. Admit 65 children. Morning taken up in Classification.

17 Admit two children. Stoves cause much inconvenience by smoking: put fires out. Examination of Scholars.

Reading. Class I. Fair, but monotonous

II. pretty good.

III fair

IV

Writing - I & II. fair. III & IV. bad.

Arithmetic. I fair, the rest a failure.

The children in class room under Mistress a few can read monosyllables: the greater part ignorant of alphabet.

Fig. 1.2 Inspection Report copied into the log book, July 1881.

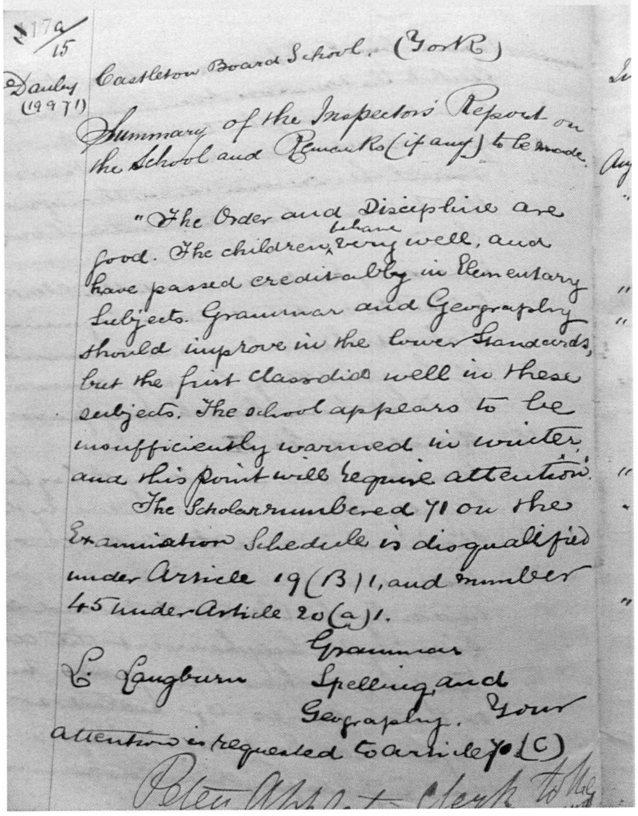

Danby (9971) Castleton Board School. (York)

Summary of the Inspector's Report on the School and Remarks (if any) to be made.

"The Order and Discipline are good. The children behave very well, and have passed creditably in Elementary Subjects. Grammar and Geography should improve in the lower Standards, but the first class did well in these subjects. The school appears to be insufficiently warmed in winter, and this point will require attention."

The Scholar numbered 71 on the Examination Schedule is disqualified under Article 19(B)1, and number 45 under Article 20(a)1.

L. Langburn

Grammar Spelling and Geography. Your attention is requested to Article 70(C)

January 7th 1875 *Stoves for the first time sufficiently heat the room.*
January 8th 1875 *Room very dark, impossible to see to write in Copy books.*
November 22nd 1876 *No sewing today, school too dark.*
November 23rd 1877 *Needlework in abeyance during the dark season.*

In early 1875 examinations were held. As the children had only been at school for a matter of weeks we should not be unduly surprised by the results.

January 28th 1875 *Examination held. Arithmetic Standards I and IV bad. Spelling Standards I and V very poor. Reading of Standard III a very weak point.*

A couple of months later the head teacher tested Standard V on the geography of the British Isles. He remarked: *with indifferent results.*

The following year the children's geography lessons had included the wider world but they must not have been paying attention:

July 5th 1876 *Examined Standards V and VI in the geography of Africa – not well up.*

Mr Bull appears to have been an unsatisfactory head master. On October 8th 1877, following the half-term Harvest Holiday, the school reopened with few children. On December 10th of that year the record tells us that Mr Banks took charge of the school at a fixed salary of £105 per year. He recorded that the school was in a very disorderly state, that writing was poor throughout and that the summary of attendance was not to be found.

Mr Banks also seems to have been surprised as to how little the children understood.

January 25th 1878 In Standard II only 3 out of 19 pupils could work out the sums 10.021 + 41.72, 25 + 309 and 18031 + 9426. In Standard III out of 10 pupils none could do £10.6s.9d - £1.7s.10d or 1s 7d - 17d. Results miserable.

Sadly this second head master was as unsatisfactory as the first and he was reported as being unfit for his post. On October 31st 1879 he tendered his resignation and a temporary head was appointed for one month until Mr Thomas Gillibrand came to the school on December 1st.

Mr Gillibrand also noted the freezing conditions within the school.

January 19th 1880 Took each class in turn around the fire.
January 26th 1880 School unfit to be in on account of the cold.

Mr Gillibrand made several complaints to the Board about the cold conditions within the school but to no avail. However, he does seem to have made an impression on the children and standards began to improve.

June 28th 1880 Exam results very good. Much improved on last year and not equalled in former years. Began the new year's work with better spirits.

Mr Gillibrand must have felt he had an uphill struggle. One of the early Inspection Reports on the school records that it was *insufficiently warmed in winter* (Fig. 1.2).

The following year the head master recorded:

June 27th 1881 Well satisfied with exam results considering the winter and the many other obstacles thrown in the way of successful teaching both by the Board and the parents.

But the light levels within the school continued to give problems.

November 30th 1881 Had to close at 3.30 on three afternoons owing to darkness.

If the light was a problem then the heating was even more so.

Mr Bull, Mr Banks and Mr Gillibrand had all complained to the Board about the temperature in the school. Sometimes the classroom was full of smoke, and Mr Gillibrand had taught around the fire and complained about the freezing temperatures within the building. Finally, on February 13th 1882 a new stove arrived and was fitted one week later. But that was not the end of the matter.

February 20th 1882 10.15 a.m. the stove set fire to the floor. Sent for Clerk and Treasurer and put out the fire.
March 3rd 1882 Stove smoked very much.

Perhaps it is not surprising that one of the next entries reads:

March 6th 1882 Standards II and III very dull this week, especially in arithmetic.

Irregular attendance by many of the children must have made it difficult to keep track of pupils' progress. There was also a need to impress on parents the importance of their children attending school regularly if they were to benefit from it. In an entry in November of 1884 Mr Gillibrand records:

Decided to prosecute James Raw for letting his daughter run about the street instead of being at school.

But even when children did attend school it seems that they did not always make progress.

March 17th 1886 Progress in all standards good except IV and nothing seems to move it. Kept them in from play and also gave home lessons but no impression for the better seems to have been made. Mrs Gillibrand also tried with them but gave them up as hopeless.

In June of 1888 Mr Gillibrand resigned as the head master and Mr Walker was appointed. His task was made all the more difficult as Mr Gillibrand opened a private school in the village taking about 20 of the Castleton Board School children. The venture was short lived, however, and his school closed by the end of the year with the children returning to the Board School. This suggests that Mr Gillibrand had done no better than his two predecessors and one of Mr Walker's early comments seems to support this.

August 24th 1888 *Had to commence with the very elements of geography as the children had not the slightest idea of even the use and meaning of a map.*

The following year Mr Walker was already beginning to grow weary:

April 12th 1889 *Nothing of note to record except that William Milner's composition* (story writing) *appears to grow worse.*

It must be remembered of course that most of these children had not been to school before. Some of them may have attended a 'dame school' and been taught to read by one of the ladies in the village or perhaps by their parents but for most of them school probably seemed rather like a prison and there were many other things to distract them from their studies.

While schools had been set up to deal with the three Rs – Reading, wRiting and 'Rithmetic – for many rural children of the nineteenth century, life was more to do with the three Hs – Haytime, Harvest and Housework. Many school hours were lost as the children had to help with jobs around the farm and garden or do household chores. Sometimes they had to leave school altogether to 'go to place' to bring in much needed income. Their 'place' would have been a larger household where they would have to work for long hours for little pay but would have 'all found', that is they would be fed and have a place to sleep.

May 14th 1875 *Mary Scarth withdrawn; gone to place.*
May 17th 1875 *Elizabeth Scarth withdrawn; gone to service.*
March 26th 1877 *John Bennison left, going to Stockton to place.*

Sometimes the children were given permission to have time off school to help with work on the farms.

June 1st 1875 *Alfred Dale has leave of absence for 2 days to collect turf.*
July 7th 1875 *John Underwood and Robert Coverdale have leave of absence for haymaking.*
July 27th 1875 *John and Thomas Raw absent helping their father to collect bark.*
July 21st 1876 *Average low on account of hay making.*
October 10th 1876 *Boys engaged in potato picking.*
May 29th 1877 *G Duck and J Longburne planting potatoes.*
June 28th 1878 *Several of the children away working in gardens and hay making.*

And sometimes the entries make amusing reading.

October 17th 1884 *Attendance only fair on account of potato gathering and diarrhoea.*

And it wasn't always farm work that kept children from their lessons.

August 10th 1876 *Isaac Taylor has leave to stay at home to nurse a sick child.*
October 27th 1876 *Annual cheese fair – several boys absent in consequence.*
October 25th 1878 *Cheese fair – attendance in the afternoon low.*
May 10th 1880 *Several children absent – cleaning for Whitsuntide.*
December 1880 *Children usually kept at home just before Christmas to help with cleaning.*

Sometimes it was the head master himself who caused interruptions to education.

October 2nd 1876 *A boy sent round to look for absentees.*
November 18th 1876 *Sent boys out to collect ling for the stoves.*
July 19th 1878 *School dismissed an hour early as boys to go to the moor for ling.*

It must have been difficult to plan lessons with so many interruptions. Children would also have been absent in order to attend local events and sometimes the head teacher simply had to give in to these and close the school as there would be so few children in attendance.

June 28th 1875 *Children given an afternoon's holiday as there was a procession of Oddfellows in the village.*
September 28th 1875 *Half holiday on account of Harvest Home at Westerdale.*
September 29th 1875 *Danby Harvest Festival: a half holiday in the afternoon.*
August 17th 1876 *A holiday, being the Cattle Show Day.*
June 13th 1877 *Wesleyan Sunday School trip.*
February 14th 1889 *A fox let loose in the village this afternoon and no school in consequence.*
July 25th 1890 *So few children attending school as out haymaking, school closed Tuesday, Wednesday and Thursday.*

Sometimes even the school Board had a hand in disrupting lessons.

February 18th 1889 *Board gave a holiday as hounds met at Westerdale.*

And sometimes the children absented themselves even if they weren't given permission.

February 15th 1878 *Eskdale Hounds met – with the exception of one or two boys the whole of Classes 1 & 2 absent.*
June 6th 1879 *Many away for Danby School feast.*
August 29th 1879 *Many children are only attending half time. Attendance at Danby and Fryup Schools is 75% above that at Castleton.*
June 27th 1881 *Several children absent on account of Primitive Methodists' trip to Saltburn.*
December 5th 1881 *Boys absent at pigeon shooting match. Master sent to enquire of parents if they knew – some did, some did not.*
October 15th 1883 *Several absent this afternoon owing to the Harvest Home Service and free tea party at Westerdale.*

Occasionally of course the school closures were scheduled and were part of national celebrations.

May 24th 1892 *Holiday for the Queen's birthday.*

Inevitably, in the days before the National Health Service and national vaccination programmes, some serious health issues also affected attendance.

December 3rd 1875 *Half of the school absent due to scarlet fever.*
December 4th 1875 *School closed by order of the Board due to scarlet fever.*
September 25th 1876 *Fred Holmes has diphtheria.*
January 18th 1878 *Robert Coverdale returned having been absent since last July.*
April 25th 1879 *An outbreak of whooping cough.*
March 1881 *An outbreak of whooping cough.*
May 1881 *Several children have measles.*
January 8th 1883 *School reopened – attendance poor due to sickness.*
February 16th 1883 *Children very sluggish, probably caused by the measles.*
January 28th 1890 *School closed due to an outbreak of measles.*
February 14th 1890 *School disinfected.*
February 17th 1890 *School reopened.*

In 1891 there was an outbreak of influenza closely followed by one of scarletina (scarlet fever).

There are also records of particularly sad news.

> March 13th 1876 *Rachel Coverdale, a promising girl at school on Friday 10th, died on Sunday morning 12th March.*
>
> March 17th 1876 *Panic over the fever therefore school closed for 10 weeks until June 4th.*
>
> June 21st 1878 *Elizabeth Watson, a scholar in Standard II, has died. Many of the children attended the funeral.*

In February of the following year the head master made this entry:

> February 7th 1879 *Many of the children want looking after.*

A comment three years later gives an indication of how much the children needed looking after.

> July 14th 1882 *Commenced school this morning at 8.45 so as to close earlier to allow the children from a distance to go home for dinner and to wash themselves ready for the inspection this afternoon.*

Local weather conditions affected numbers, as they can still do so today, although some of the entries do indicate that winters were much more severe than they are now.

> December 24th 1874 *Just 25 children present owing to stormy weather, school closed for one week for the Christmas holiday.*
>
> November 12th 1878 *Heavy fall of snow, doors blocked up, roads impassable, only 5 scholars in attendance.*
>
> October 14th 1881 *Terrible storm at its height at 3.30. Several came to help to get the children home. Slates taken off roofs, one complete window and frame blown right out, later found at High Castleton and returned by Mrs Watson. Rain fell in torrents, penetrated the walls and poured through the roof. Beds in the house wet through.*

The head master records he *procured lodgings* as the house was unfit to sleep in. That evening the doors were nailed up and windows boarded. The school was closed the following week and when it opened attendance was poor as many of the children were afraid to go to school.

> November 30th 1881 *Had to close school at 3.30 on three afternoons as it was so dark.*
>
> December 9th 1883 *School closed as slates dangerous after overnight gales and windows broken by tiles falling from next door roof as well as the large gate taken from its hinges.*
>
> March 1st 1889 *Mr Kitching sent a sledge and took the children home noon and night.*
>
> April 28th 1892 *School closed due to severe snow storm and gales.*
>
> January 25th 1895 *Hurricane force winds, even strong men were blown to the ground.*

From the beginning there were the behaviour issues familiar to any teacher.

> February 17th 1875 *Boys cautioned against playing in the Girls' Watercloset* (toilets) *during dinner time.*
>
> April 21st 1875 *First Class boys kept in till 5 p.m. for staying out after school hours had begun.*
>
> August 3rd 1876 *Boys cautioned against playing in the girls' playground.*
>
> May 9th 1877 *Girls cautioned about defacing the walls of the water closets.*
>
> May 10th 1878 *Gave one stripe each across the shoulders for stubbornness to three boys.*
>
> March 28th 1879 *Jane Scarth of Commondale stole M Sanderson's purse with 1/- in it. She spent a penny before being found out. 11d returned to M Sanderson.*
>
> June 18th 1883 *J E Suggitt punished for impudence. She at once threw down her knitting and went home. When spoken to or told to do anything this child's reply has generally been 'no I shan't, you can't make me and if you give me the cane my Dada will come and give it to you.' Kept her in one day at noon to finish a lesson but her mother came and took her away saying she would neither have her kept in nor punished with the cane.*

Sometimes the issues were slightly more serious.

> June 15th 1876 *A complaint having been made of stone throwing and using of catapults, the policeman was called in to warn boys of the consequences attending the practice.*
> August 3rd 1877 *Boys prohibited from playing a game called 'codlings'*[2] *on account of the danger to themselves and school property.*

With many of the early log book entries relating to behaviour, the weather, absences or practical issues to do with the school building, it is difficult to get a true picture of what the lessons looked like. Fortunately, two late nineteenth-century school exercise books have survived, now in the possession of Jacqueline Chapman (née Medd). These were completed by Dora Duck between October 1889 and January 1891. It would appear that Dora was aged 11 and 12 during this period so would have been one of the oldest pupils at the school. From these books we can see that Mr Walker, the head teacher when Dora was completing her exercise books, seems to have been a much better teacher than the first three. In the log book, he does begin to record what he was teaching and Dora's exercise books bear this out. He taught the children about types of sentences and gave them dictated passages to write but seems to have concentrated more on arithmetic and geography. The children had one exercise book for all subjects so composition, grammar, mathematics, history and geography all appear within its pages. Dora's handwriting is very neat, written with pen and ink of course. Most of her arithmetic is correct and the books include some well drawn and detailed maps. It is also interesting to note that whenever she leaves even just four lines at the bottom of a page the head master comments on the waste of paper (Fig. 1.3). The books are a fascinating glimpse into a nineteenth-century elementary school as well as some aspects of village life. Some of Dora's work even suggests that Victorian teachers were not as straight-laced as we have sometimes been led to believe.

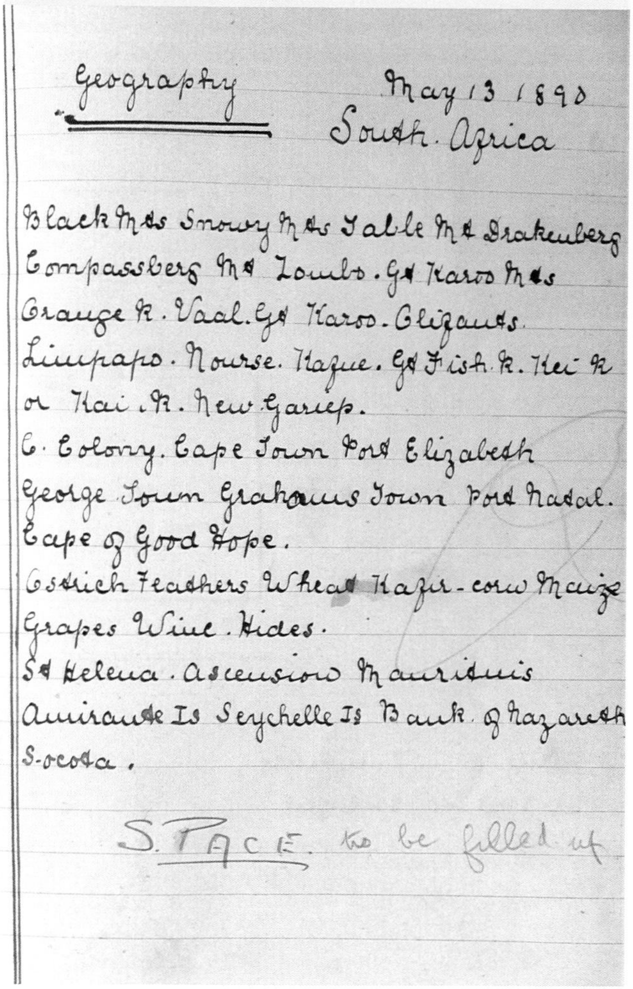
Geography May 13 1890
South Africa
Black Mts Snowy Mts Table Mt Drakenberg
Compassberg Mt Zoulo. Gt Karoo Mts
Orange R. Vaal. Gt Karoo. Olifants
Limpapo. Nourse. Hague. Gt Fish R. Kei R
or Kai R. New Gariep.
C. Colony. Cape Town Port Elizabeth
George Town Grahams Town Port Natal.
Cape of Good Hope.
Ostrich Feathers Wheat Kafir-corn Maize
Grapes Wine. Hides.
St Helena. Ascension Mauritius
Amirante Is Seychelle Is Bank of Nazareth
Socotra.
SPACE to be filled up

Fig. 1.3 Page from the exercise book of Dora Duck, May 13th 1890.

One written exercise, which appears to have been dictated to the class on October 5th 1889, reads:[3]

> *A gentleman living some distance from London had a season ticket for the railway. Coming through the stations so often he thought the servants of the railway would know him. A porter came to see the tickets. As the gentleman did not show his ticket the porter said sharply "Tickets, sir." The gentleman, a great man in his own estimation, replied "My face is my ticket." "Indeed sir," said the porter, rolling up his sleeve and showing a large and powerful fist. "Well my orders are to punch all tickets passing through this station. Hold it up."*

And on November 6th of the same year:

> *A gentleman with a glass eye on his arrival in India engaged a numerous staff of servants among which was a man who had to fan his master through the night. The gentleman was amused at hearing the conversation of his servants as*

Pages of arithmetic from Dora Duck's exercise books.

Fig. 1.4

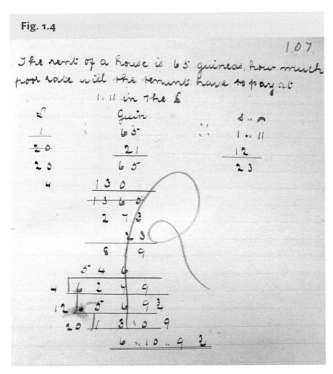

Fig. 1.5

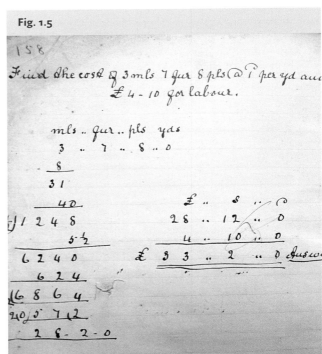

Fig. 1.6

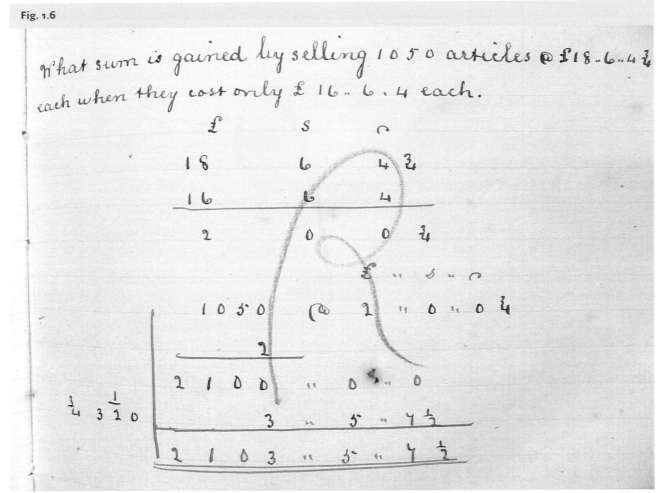

Fig. 1.7 Hand-drawn map of Europe.

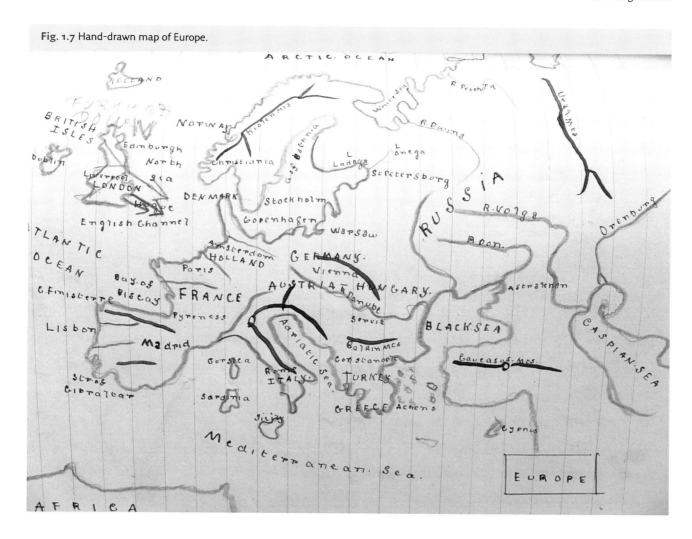

one of them said, "Ah my master is a sly fox he takes one of his eyes out and lays it upon the table and I have to fan him till the other eye wakes up."

Just a few days later Dora wrote:

A Dentist was once engaged to pull a labours[4] tooth out, which was giving him much pain. He was asked to take a seat and he had hardly sat down when the tooth was out. The man asked him how much it was and the Dentist said "I cannot charge a labouring man the full fee I shall be satisfied with half a crown." The man said, "Half a crown? Why you don't mean it! I had one pulled out with a doctor and he pulled me all over the room and he only charged a shilling."

Another of Dora's pieces of writing gives us a clear picture of what life was like for a child before television, electronic devices and all of the other trappings of our twenty-first century world. In October 1889 she wrote:

On Saturday before breakfast I (cleaned?) my own boots & afterwards went to shop for mother. I clean the knives and forks and afterwards sweep the yard weeded the garden and swept the paths. Afterwards chop sticks for the fire. Soon after dinner I go out to play in summer, play at cricket, in winter football and rounders, or some such game. After tea I learn my lessons for Sunday School. I read a book, put scraps in books or play games with my sisters.

Sunday. I light the fire & after breakfast I get ready for Church & after service I get my dinner. Afterwards I read and then get ready for Sunday School. We sing hymns & have a lesson & then go home. I get the tea ready & then go for a walk with father & mother & sisters. They go to Church I stay at home with my sisters and read & sing till bed time.

Similarly in June 1890 she wrote:

Dora Duck, date unknown but *circa* 1900.

My Saturdays and how I spend them
I get up about six o'clock wash myself and get my breakfast.
When we finish I wash up and then I begin to work and get done
about one o'clock. Then I get washed and go out for a walk and
gather wild flowers in the woods. When I come back I get my tea
and wash up and then go and have about an hours practice.[5]
Afterwards I go for a walk or go for a row in the boat. I then
have my supper, go for another practice and go to bed.

The work in the book is marked VG, for very good, or R, for right, written across the work in blue crayon. Most of the arithmetic is marked with blue Rs. Sums such as:

The rent of a house is 65 guineas, how much poor rate will the
tenant have to pay at 1/11 in the £. (Fig. 1.4)
Find the cost of 3mls 7 fur 8 pls at 1d per yard and £4 10s for labour. (Fig. 1.5)
What sum is gained by selling 1050 articles @ £18 6s 4¾d each when they cost only £16 6s 4d each. (Fig. 1.6)

Geography seems to have been a regular lesson. On Friday 11th July 1890 Mr Walker wrote that *maps of Europe have had a share of interest.* This is evident in Dora's exercise book where she has copied a map of Europe (Fig 1.7). The children also learnt a great deal about the British Empire, especially India (Figs. 1.8, 1.9, 1.10 & 1.11). The two maps of India were completed in March and October 1890 and it is possible to see Dora's progress in her map drawing skills over those months. She closes her first exercise book with a very detailed map of the world (Fig. 1.12).

Several times in her exercise books, Dora writes the name M Appleton at the top of the page. On Friday July 18th 1890, Mr Walker records that Mrs Walker was unwell and that *M Appleton assisted.* On August 15th he records that Mrs Appleton spoke to him about her daughter, May (or Mary), becoming a Pupil Teacher. It is likely that May was still in her teens at the time. On January 9th 1891 the log book tells us that once again Mrs Walker was unwell and *Mary Appleton assisted during the week.* She would have been supervising the youngest children, probably reading stories to them and helping them to count.

The log book and Dora's exercise books suggest that Mr Walker was trying to widen the horizons of these village children, to make sure that they could write clearly and do the arithmetic that was necessary to manage in their nineteenth-century environment. Nevertheless, all of the records of the early years of the school at Castleton suggest that conditions within the school were far from ideal, that it was not easy to get the children to attend regularly, and that the first three head masters were not up to the task. In spite of Mr Walker's best efforts attendance continued to be erratic, especially of the older children who were needed to do vital work out of school. From 1892, however, that began to change when Mr Groves was appointed as head master. His early remarks are about the children not knowing their multiplication tables and that their writing was *slip-shod* with a lot of late-coming but he clearly intended to change all of that.

NOTES

1   The log book entries are recorded throughout this book exactly as they were first written.
2   Codlings is a game similar to cricket.
3   Dora's work is recorded here exactly as it first appears in her exercise books.
4   The dictation was obviously 'labourer's'.
5   Dora does not record what she was practising but it was probably the piano.

Fig. 1.8 Hand-drawn map of parts of the British Empire.

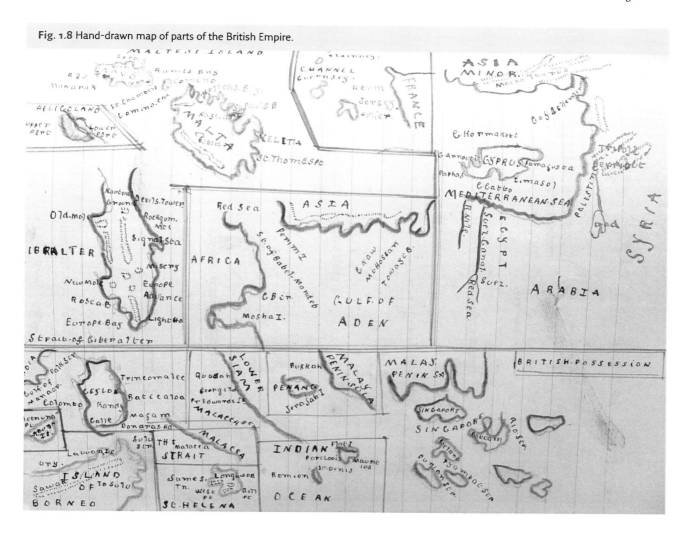

Fig. 1.9 Map of India drawn March 1890.

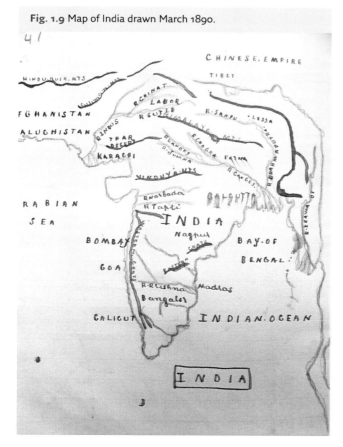

Fig. 1.10 Notes on India.

India

India is 1900 miles from north to south and 1800 miles from east to west. The shores are washed by the Bay of Bengal on the east and Arabian Sea on the west. It is not intended by gulfs or bay except in the north west. An English company of trading men began in 1600. In 1664 a French East India Company was formed there was great rivalry between the two companies for many years. There were many petty contests the great victory of the English at Plassey under Lord Clive (1757) The possessions of the English increased during the next 100 years. In 1857 a terrible mutiny in the native army hundreds of English men women and children were cruelly murdered and their property was destroyed In 1876 Queen Victoria was proclaimed Empress of India.

Fig. 1.11 Map of India drawn October 1890.

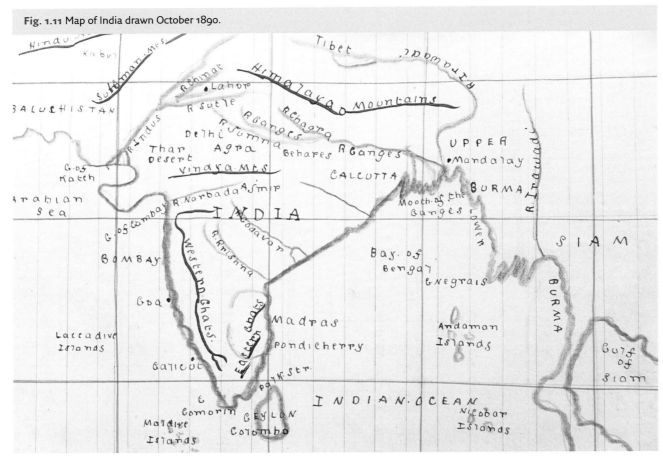

Fig. 1.12 Map of the world drawn April 1890.

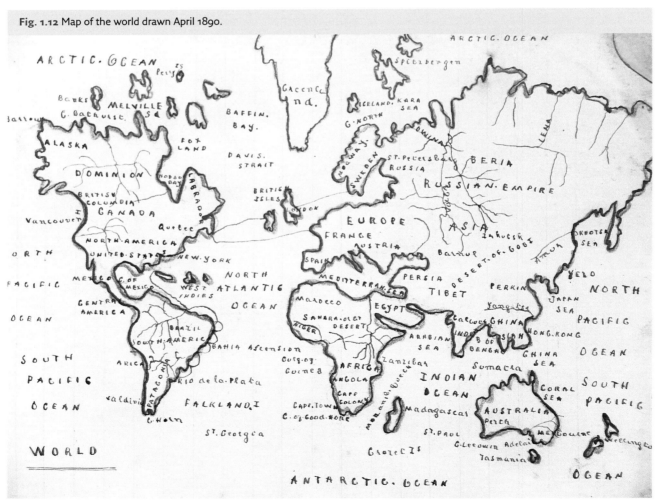

CHAPTER 2

The Headship of Mr Groves

M R GROVES was to stay at the school for nearly thirty years until his death in September 1921. Although he also continued to record absence, difficulties with the stove, problems with the weather and illness of the children he was clearly a dedicated teacher who wanted the best for his pupils. Within his first year at the school he was recording details of some of the lessons. For instance for the academic year 1893 – 94 the children were learning about:

The lion, the fox, fish, sugar, coffee, iron, silver, needles, candles, the railway, the post office, seasons, sun, moon and stars, lifeboats and blacksmiths.

At the end of May 1893 the inspection report reads:

I am glad to report a decided improvement both in the tone and discipline of the school.

Very soon Mrs Groves was teaching the infants while Mr Groves taught the older children. They must have been a good team. Two years later the inspection report records:

The infants are much better trained and taught than is usual in schools of this class.

Fig. 2.1 The earliest known photograph of Castleton School *circa* 1895. Note the girls' long dresses and the boys' Eton collars. The slate, bottom centre, records this as Castleton Council School. (The original fragments are stuck behind broken picture glass.)

The survival of part of a late nineteenth-century photograph suggests that Mr Groves arranged for the school to be put on record early in his headship (Fig. 2.1). This picture of just 26 children, at a time when there were more than 80 on roll, gives a clear indication of the degree of absence in those days.

Sadly ill health continued to be an issue affecting the school.

> March 9th 1894 *Pupil Richard Milner died.*
> March 13th 1894 *School closed for the funeral.*
> October 25th 1895 *Nettie Marsay, an infant, died of diphtheria. The Doctor advises that scholars are not taken to the funeral.*
> December 1895 *An epidemic of "sore throat", 30 children excluded, average attendance only 39.*

The school was disinfected over the Christmas holiday.

In spite of absence, illness and on-going problems with light levels as well as the infamous stove, Mr Groves was determined to improve the education of the local children. In October 1897 he recorded that he had started to give special attention to those needing extra help with arithmetic and he was also starting to run evening classes. The following year an additional member of staff was appointed:

June 7th 1898 *Miss Nina M Simpson appointed infant teacher.*

Miss Simpson stayed at the school for just two years and was replaced by Miss Martha Appleton in October 1900.

With the arrival of an infant teacher, Mrs Groves became the sewing mistress. Needlework would have been taught at the school since it was opened. It was an important part of school life at a time when most women had to make, and often mend, their own clothes. The girls would learn basic sewing techniques as well as creating a book of samplers of types of seams, embroidery stitches and darning patterns. A local sampler book from the early years of the twentieth century has survived. This was made at Westerdale School but similar stitches would have been practised at Castleton (Figs. 2.2 – 2.7).

By the opening year of the twentieth century there were 105 children on the school roll but the average attendance was still only 76. In November 1900 Mr Groves recorded that some days only 50 children attended school so regular absence was still a problem. However, his teaching was beginning to make a difference.

> June 7th 1901 *On May 30th a lecturer of the Band of Hope Union of Yorkshire delivered a lecture "Alcohol and its effects upon the Human Body." 20 children subsequently sent in essays. All of them received a certificate of merit for their work, 2 children achieving 95%. The lecturer wrote "The work done by your pupils reflects great credit upon their training. I am more than gratified."*

By the turn of the twentieth century Mr Groves also seems to have been making the children more aware of national events.

> January 23rd 1901 *On Wednesday Mr Meggeson, chairman of the school board, visited school. The Master had just concluded addressing the scholars upon the death of Her Most Gracious Majesty, Queen Victoria, and the Chairman added a few kindly expressions to what had already been said.*
> March 8th 1901 *In accordance with a circular issued by the Board of Education, a lesson was given this afternoon upon the coming census.*
> October 16th 1901 *School closed – procession and public reception of Captain the Honourable John Dawnay returning from the South African war.*
> February 14th 1902 *Children taught "God Save our Gracious King".*
> June 2nd 1902 *News arrived that peace declared in South Africa, school closed for the afternoon.*
> June 27th 1902 *Coronation celebrations – sudden illness of the King therefore no holiday.*

Fig. 2.2 Beatrice Emma Hartley's initials embroidered on her work in chain stitch.

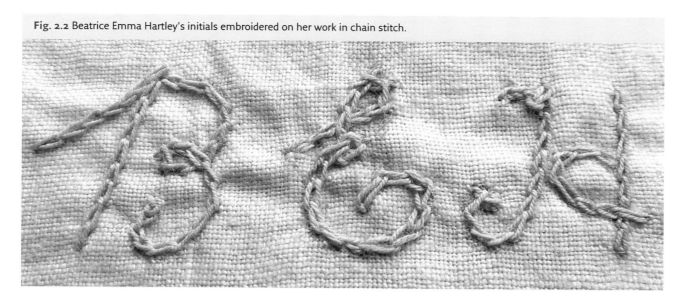

Fig. 2.3 A fine seam sewn *circa* 1910.

Fig. 2.4 A finely stitched and embroidered opening for a garment.

Fig. 2.5 Embroidery detail. The straight stitches are very fine at 20 to the inch.

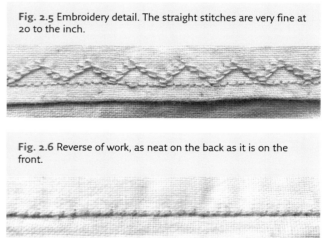

Fig. 2.6 Reverse of work, as neat on the back as it is on the front.

Fig. 2.7 A vented opening stitched by Beatrice Hartley at Westerdale School *circa* 1910.

We also start to hear of a few more treats for the children.

> August 7th 1902 *School closed for the summer holiday. The King's expressed wish – an extra week's holiday. Medallion boxes of chocolates for each child.*
> December 20th 1901 *All the children given an orange from the chairman, Mr Kitching.*
> December 23rd 1904 *Children given a handkerchief each as a Christmas present.*

Occasionally the entries in the log book tell us a bit more about the school itself and some of the issues to do with education at that time.

> January 3rd 1903 *Gallery removed and floor made level.*
> January 23rd 1903 *At Wednesday's Board meeting the unsual incident occurred of a member objecting to a number of pictures being purchased to illustrate object lessons during the current year's work. His plea was that owing to the passing of the Education Act the Board would shortly go out of existence.*
> June 17th 1903 *Last meeting of Danby School Board.* (They would now be called managers.)

And even more telling:

> October 16th 1903 *School materials ordered in July came to hand on Wednesday!*
> September 29th 1905 *Girls' cloakroom in use after alterations and boiler ceiling plastered.*
> May 18th 1906 *Dual desks arrived for upper standards.*

The managers' minute book also provides some interesting details from this period.

November 6th 1903

Whitby Gas C. truck of coke	£3 14s 8d
Mr Appleton for leading coke and goods from station	9s 0d
	£4 3s 8d

Unfortunately, no exercise books seem to have survived but there is a second school photograph from this period. This appears to have been taken at the turn of the century with the mistress in a long, dark skirt and the boys in their Eton collars, both of which began to go out of fashion after 1918 (Fig. 2.8) With just 36 children on the school photograph this again is by no means all of those on the roll but those attending that day. A photograph of Mr and Mrs Groves and their son is also shown (Fig. 2.9).

By July 1904 there were 109 children on roll – a very full school indeed.
Mr Groves had clearly been trying to increase the level of attendance for some time.

> August 8th 1901 *George Flintoft, among others, received a book as prize for attending school all year.*

Eventually this was to take effect.

> June 4th 1907 *Every scholar (103) present, a circumstance unique at this school.*

Sadly this was not to last.

> February 28th 1908 *Continued absence and irregularity is making the work in school extremely difficult.*

However, Mr Groves' teaching methods do seem to have been recognised.

> October 4th 1907 *Miss Hartley of Westerdale School attended here all day on Wednesday by sanction of the County Education Committee to observe methods in use.*

And not all of the lessons were in the classroom.

September 16th 1910 *Older children taken out for a ramble, found sundew and butterwort.*

Fig. 2.8 School photograph *circa* 1900.

Illness and major national events continued to make their appearance within the records.

January 1911 *A fatal case of diphtheria during the Christmas holidays. Scholars in the houses either side excluded from school, average attendance low.*

March 17th 1911 *Children taught about the census.*

June 19th 1911 *School closed for the whole week for the coronation of George V.*

December 1911 *Outbreak of diphtheria.*

In spite of all of his hard work at the school it seems that it was difficult for Mr Groves to get any home improvements made. The managers' minute book records:

October 1911 *Mr Groves requested a bath for the school house. It was moved that the managers do not make the recommendation asked for. Carried unanimously with 2 abstentions.*

Just three years later some of the entries take on a more sinister nature.

October 2nd 1914 *Seven old scholars have joined the army.*

May 2nd 1916 *Zeppelins passed over the village.*

September 8th 1916 *Joseph Thompson killed accidently, first old scholar to fall.*

October 4th 1917 *Old scholar "straight from the Western Front" looked into school. Had been wounded in the head.*

September 27th 1918 *Tom Robinson, on leave from the Western Front, visited school. In the army since September 1914.*

At last the war came to an end but only to be followed by a devastating epidemic.

November 15th 1918 *School closed in honour of the end of the war. Influenza epidemic.*

November 19th 1918 *School closed due to epidemic.* December 13th 1918 *School reopened after 3 weeks.*

It was another year before there is a record of peace celebrations.

December 12th 1919 *Last Saturday scholars treated to a tea at Ainthorpe School by the Peace Celebrations Committee and were presented with a "Peace" goblet and a shilling.*

The log book entries continue to touch on national as well as local events. British Summer Time (BST) had been introduced during the war years with the passing of the Summer Time Act in 1916. BST continued after the ceasing of hostilities and was seen to be affecting children's attendance at school. The following entry might sound familiar.

May 7th 1920 *The children are allowed to stay up too late on a night, quite young children are not going to bed until 10 pm, consequently they are late on a morning or are tired and sleepy until noon.*

Fig. 2.9 Mr and Mrs Groves and their son.

Mr Groves records yet another outbreak of diphtheria in October 1920 with one child dying as a consequence. His handwriting then begins to deteriorate and the record tells us:

March 4th 1921 *Master temporarily excused duty for two months.*

In May of that year Mr Dale was appointed as temporary head master with Mrs Groves keeping the logbook. She makes a very poignant entry.

September 9th 1921 *Mrs M Groves was absent today owing to the death of my husband on Thursday evening – head master of this school since June 1892.*

This must have been a very sad day for the school and the whole community. Mr and Mrs Groves had been at the school for 29 years. The managers' minute book records:

September 9th 1921 *A Resolution of Sympathy was moved by the Chair who, in feeling terms, expressed himself unequal to the task of adequately speaking of the great loss the school had sustained. Mr Groves was a schoolmaster in every sense of the word. Members rose in their places.*

Mr and Mrs Groves had improved the teaching standards as well as the attendance, seen the introduction of an assistant teacher for the infants and overseen several practical improvements to the building. Their contribution to Castleton School is here acknowledged as a tremendous achievement. We are all grateful for their hard work and dedication.

CHAPTER 3

Between the Wars and Immediate Post-War Years

IN JANUARY 1922 Mr Jackson was appointed as head master. He soon joined the ranks of those complaining about the heating system and other facilities at the school.

February 3rd 1922 *I consider the heating apparatus defective and insufficient for the school.*
February 4th 1922 *Wrote to Northallerton with regard to the appalling state of the out offices – boys' door hanging off, girls' a constant quagmire, atmosphere constantly poisoned.*

It is clear from the log book that conditions within the school continued to be far from ideal.

November 9th 1923 *Temperature in the school just 47°F (8°C).*
November 16th 1923 *Fire regularly going out.*
December 10th 1923 *Infant room just 37°F (3°C) at 9 a.m.*
May 29th 1924 *Inspection of the heating system.*
July 4th 1924 *Work began on the heating system.*

Unfortunately, this was not the end of the issue of the stove.

October 10th 1924 *Problems with the stove. One day the caretaker lit it at 5 a.m. and then forgot about it.*
April 22nd 1926 *No fire as fuel ran out.*
November 25th 1926 *Several days without fuel. Temperature in school 39°F (4°C).*
December 7th 1926 *No fire or fuel, only 20 children in school, school closed for the day.*
December 8th 1926 *11.30 a.m. coke arrived. 33 out of 75 children in school for the afternoon.*

As well as the lack of heat there were other practical problems that must have hindered teaching and learning.

March 11th 1927 *Slates blown off several weeks ago now replaced. Drain blocked and boys' playground flooded.*
April 8th 1927 *Wind from the north therefore fumes from the furnace.*
August 29th 1927 *Coke stacked in the yard as cellar roof not repaired.*

And another telling entry:

November 7th 1927 *Stock ordered in July arrived today!*

In spite of these local problems, the school was taking part in more national events.

February 8th 1922 *Penny fund for Princess Mary's wedding present, 6/6 sent. Considering the large amount of unemployment in the district the response was quite creditable.*
April 26th 1923 *School closed for the marriage of the Duke and Duchess of York.* (Later George VI and Queen Elizabeth, who subsequently became the Queen Mother.)

One school photograph has survived from the early 1920s. It is particularly interesting to note how many brothers and sisters were at the school in the days of much larger families. I have been told that there were twelve brothers and sisters in one family (Fig. 3.1)

Fig. 3.1 School photograph *circa* 1922. Mr Jackson head teacher, infant teacher unknown. Believed to be in the photograph but identity uncertain – Mary and Eva Featherstone, Winnie Cook, Phoebe Williamson, Lily and Fred Thompson, Nora, Sid and Ray Husband, Eileen and Lewis Boyes, Jack and Earnest Watson, John, Harry, Rebe and Eva Williamson, Eileen Ingledew, Bernard Annis, Percy, Annie, Jack and Nora Booth, Dora Duck, Mary Medd (second row second from left), Allen Medd (front row holding Castleton Council School board). Alan Medd later married Dora Duck. Note the grass immediately in front of the school steps.

Fig. 3.2 Church of St Michael and St George, Castleton.

Fig. 3.3 School photograph, 1925.
Back row left to right – Miss Tibble, Sarah Dale, unknown, Findleson twins, Allan Miller, Alfie Watson, Harry Thorpe, Susie Williamson, Mr Jackson.
Front row left to right - Unknown, Mary Booth, Douglas Booth, Emma Knaggs, Peggie Askew, ? Askew, Ronnie Cook, Peter Jackson, Miles Cook (known as Miley).
Note the heavy boots that some of the children are wearing, probably used by several children in the same family over a number of years.

Fig. 3.4 School photograph *circa* 1927. Infant teacher unknown, possibly Miss Laurenson.
Front row left to right – Betty Medd, Dorothy Williamson, Doris Robinson, Margaret Ellerby, Eilleen Ellerby, Joan Gray, Doris Gibson.
Second row left to right – Barry Knaggs, Jack Robinson, Susie Williamson, Greta Gray, Lilian Marsay, Mary Rose, George Ellerby, Len Scarth.
Third row left to right – John Scarth, Bill Cockerill, Ron Cook, Basil Ascomb.
Back row left to right – Ray Husband, Fred Welford, Bill Mead, Harry Thorpe.

Local conditions must have been changing following the war as in May 1923 Mr Jackson recorded that the number on roll was 57 and by May 1924 just 50. However, standards at the school continued to rise, which led to successes further afield.

June 24ᵗʰ 1924 *Henry Williamson, aged 10, awarded a Junior Scholarship tenable at Whitby County School.*
June 25ᵗʰ 1924 *John Fishpool won a prize in a national competition for an essay entitled "My Favourite Author and Why".*
December 1924 *For the second year in succession the school won first prize in the county for the best essay – entitled "Trees". John Williamson won a postal order for 10/6.*
April 6ᵗʰ 1925 *School entered the Eskdale Tournament of country and folk dancing for the first time. Achieved 83 marks and a second class certificate.*
July 20ᵗʰ 1925 *John Williamson won a special prize in an RNLI essay competition.*
December 23ʳᵈ 1925 *School won the Smith Challenge Shield, first prize in the local history section of the North Riding Rural Industries Exhibition.*
March 28ᵗʰ 1927 *Two teams entered for Eskdale Folk Dancing Tournament. Juniors 2ⁿᵈ, Seniors 1ˢᵗ Class certificate.*
April 24ᵗʰ 1927 *Dora Duck gained Gold Medal at Eskdale Tournament of Song for piano playing.*

The record also tells us of other more local events.

July 24ᵗʰ 1924 *School opened 8.30 – 11.30 and 12.30 – 2.45 on account of the ceremony of laying of the foundation stone of the memorial church at Castleton by Viscount Downe at 3 p.m.*
July 28ᵗʰ 1926 *School closed in the afternoon, consecration of Castleton Church by the Archbishop of York.* (Fig. 3.2)

And other local names were added to the roll.

> April 1st 1925 *Emma Knaggs* (now Mrs Emma Beeforth of Westerdale) *admitted with Susie Williamson and M Booth.*

Emma remembers starting at the school but wasn't there for very long as her family soon moved back to Quarry Farm in Westerdale. She also remembers that she wasn't at the school long before she had head lice! Emma recollects being reprimanded for not being able to knit but considers this unfair as she was only five years old at the time. The following day, when her mother looked out from their home further up the High Street, she saw Emma playing in the gutter. Mrs Knaggs went down to the school to see why her little girl was out in the street and Mr Jackson took her back into school. It seems that no one noticed that she wasn't in class but Emma had absented herself as she didn't want to be scolded again.

Emma still has her first school photograph, taken when she was five years old, which shows the infant class with their teacher and the head master (Fig. 3.3).

The following year, Mr Jackson became ill and resigned his post. Miss Laurenson was appointed temporary head teacher. She makes an amusing entry into the log book.

> January 28th 1926 *Miss Laurenson writes that Miss Tibble is in school today but her neck and arm are so stiff she is unable to lift the blackboard.*

There is a second photograph from this period, probably taken in 1927 when Betty Medd (now Mrs Betty Dean) started school (Fig. 3.4).

Miss Laurenson was in her temporary post for just a month. Mr Charles Renton Hay was appointed head master in February 1926. Like Mr Groves he was to be at Castleton for over twenty years. He also quickly began to make his mark on the school.

> February 1926 *The only history text books were supplied in 1903 and are very scrappy.*

The minutes of the managers' meetings record that in September 1927, Mr Hay asked permission to throw away old books. It seems that he also made a complaint about the state of the toilets. From the managers' minute book:

> September 13th 1927 *Regarding the new water system, there are concerns about the cost compared with the pail closets for the children. The managers feeling a great difficulty in coming to a decision.*

The history books may have been scrappy and the toilets far from hygienic, but the school was at least soon to have its own piano.

> December 9th 1927 *Concert for the piano fund raised £12.10s*
> July 19th 1928 *Piano secured for the school, an upright iron grand by Archibald Ramsden, second hand £21, originally 56 guineas.*

And at last attendance was improving.

> October 5th 1928 *Olive Winnifred Cook given a beautifully bound volume of Dicken's David Copperfield for eight years unbroken attendance 23/6/20 – 23/6/28.*

Later the same child was rewarded again.

> June 30th 1930 *Olive Winifred[1] Cook today completed her school life without ever having been absent for a single session. Her record is unique in the history of the school. She was presented with a toilet case and the usual certificate.*

In spite of this exemplary record, conditions within the school continued to be troublesome.

November 15ᵗʰ 1928 I have been suffering from a severe cold in the head. School frightfully draughty owing to the stupid position of the door leading to the boys' porch.

January 24ᵗʰ 1930 The school, owing to its exposed position, and defective planning, is very draughty and is, no doubt, responsible for the many colds. I myself have not been free from severe colds in the head for nearly three months.

May 9ᵗʰ 1930 Dr Gibson visited to inspect the new system in the "outer offices". He also asked about the heating and ventilation, windows on north side not made to open!

Just two months later there was severe weather to contend with.

July 21ˢᵗ 1930 Severe rain, river flooding.

July 23ʳᵈ 1930 Water is being blown under the slates of the roof and there are thin streams of water running down the walls on the north side of the school. The ceiling is dripping in many places.

July 25ᵗʰ 1930 Many bridges broken.

And yet again the heating system was causing problems.

October 3ʳᵈ 1930 Furnace not started as new top not fixed to chimney.

October 31ˢᵗ 1930 New piece fitted to stove pipe.

November 14ᵗʰ 1930 Throat problems, fumes from the stove still getting in.

Betty Dean (née Medd) remembers 'a big black thing in the middle of the big classroom'. This, no doubt, was the infamous stove that was now sending fumes into the classroom in spite of a new flue pipe.

Yet more familiar names are recorded.

November 2ⁿᵈ 1931 Derrick and Heather Champion admitted from Rosedale Abbey.

Mr Hay was soon to make a determined drive to improve the general health of the children.

September 30ᵗʰ 1932 On Monday we are inaugurating a "clean hands" campaign with the hope that we may bring about an improvement in the habits of the boys in particular and the whole school in general.

October 11ᵗʰ 1932 School nurse visited to look at heads.

December 13ᵗʰ 1932 School nurse visited and carried out routine inspection. Nurse reported the boys quite clear of any signs of vermin. A few infant girls still need attention.

Until at last:

November 2ⁿᵈ 1934 Sixth successive merit holiday (schools were awarded these for good attendance). *There have been no "stunts", no coercive measures, no threats and it would appear that parents are really beginning to realise what is their duty to their children in this respect. On the other hand we have had no infections, diseases or epidemics which fact, I am sometimes led to believe, is largely due to the good work of our school cleaner who thoroughly deserves mention here.*

The campaign obviously continued.

September 14ᵗʰ 1937 One carton of Jeyes' Sanitary Paper and one gallon of Jeyes' Liquid Disinfectant have been received.

Mr Hay also began to attend to other practical arrangements within the school.

September 24ᵗʰ 1936 Two oak tables arrived.

Fig. 3.5 Red ink entry in the log book, May 10th 1935.

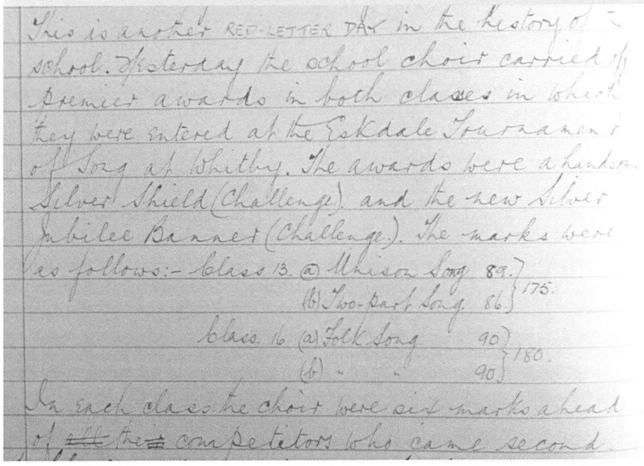
This is another RED-LETTER DAY in the history of the school. Yesterday the school choir carried off premier awards in both classes in which they were entered at the Eskdale Tournament of Song at Whitby. The awards were a handsome Silver Shield (Challenge) and the new Silver Jubilee Banner (Challenge). The marks were as follows:- Class 13. (a) Unison Song 89 (b) Two-part Song 86 } 175. Class 16 (a) Folk Song 90 (b) " 90 } 180. In each class the choir were six marks ahead of all the competitors who came second

October 16th 1936 *Six new desks and two chairs arrived.*
November 23rd 1938 *New floor put down in large classroom.*
August 28th 1939 *Start of new term. New floor in infants' room during the holidays.*

But lessons clearly weren't only in the classroom.

November 17th 1936 *Boys taken to the local garage for a demonstration on the working of the internal combustion engine.*

Perhaps it was lighter in the garage.

November 26th 1936 *Lighting of the school during the winter months is a serious menace to the eyesight of the children.*

Other entries continue to raise a smile.

March 19th 1937 *Three candidates to sit the second part of the Minor Exhibition Examination – two to sit at Lealholm tomorrow but the third is suffering from boils and is unable to sit.*

Numbers at the school had been falling during this time, consequently there was going to be a staff reduction. Mr Hay recorded this with dismay.

March 5th 1937 *There is to be a reduction in staff due at Easter. This is disastrous, after so much care has been given to the building up of the work on a three-teacher basis.*

However, the school did gain a student teacher for a time.

February 22nd 1937 *Mr Chas Hartley has been given permission by the Education Secretary to come to the school for the purposes of observation and teaching practice. Mr Hartley will enter St John's College, York in Sept. He has commenced observation work this morning.*
March 12th 1937 *Mr Hartley has given two science lessons this week and shows much promise as a teacher.*
March 25th 1937 *Miss B Leeming left today on reduction of staff.*

In spite of this reduction in staff, the school went on to win an award at the Eskdale Tournament of Song. Castleton first entered this event in 1925. In April 1934 the school had secured third place overall in the 'schools under 100' class, winning the Challenge Medal and Certificate. In 1935 the school came second, winning the Silver Shield and the Silver Jubilee Banner, an achievement which Mr Hay recorded in red ink in the log book (Fig. 3.5). The school appears not to have won a place in 1936 so there must have been much celebration the following year.

May 5th 1937 *School closed at 3.45 p.m. for the Eskdale Tournament of Song.*
May 7th 1937 *The school choir succeeded in winning the Challenge Banner for Folk Songs together with two First Class Certificates at the ETS.* (Fig. 3.6)

Staffing continued to be a problem. With even more dismay, Mr Hay records County Hall's solution:

May 5th 1938 *Miss Hilda Agar aged 18 arrived to take charge of the infants and be responsible for needlework. 3 months experience with juniors and none whatever with infants.*
January 9th 1939 *Miss Bannister, aged 20, teaching infants.*

Fig. 3.6 School photograph taken in 1937 to celebrate winning the Eskdale Tournament of Song Banner for Folk Songs. On the left Miss May Dowson, infant teacher, on the right Mr Charles Renton Hay, head teacher, with Mr Charles Hartley, student teacher.

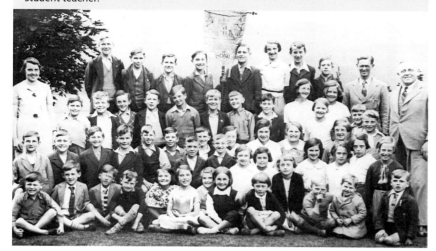

Fig. 3.6a Mr Hartley returned to the district for his war-time marriage to Joan Rudsdale of Congrave Farm, Ainthorpe. He went on to teach at Pickering, then at Stokesley.

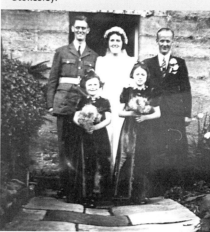

Fig. 3.7 Page from the log book of 1940 showing class attendance.

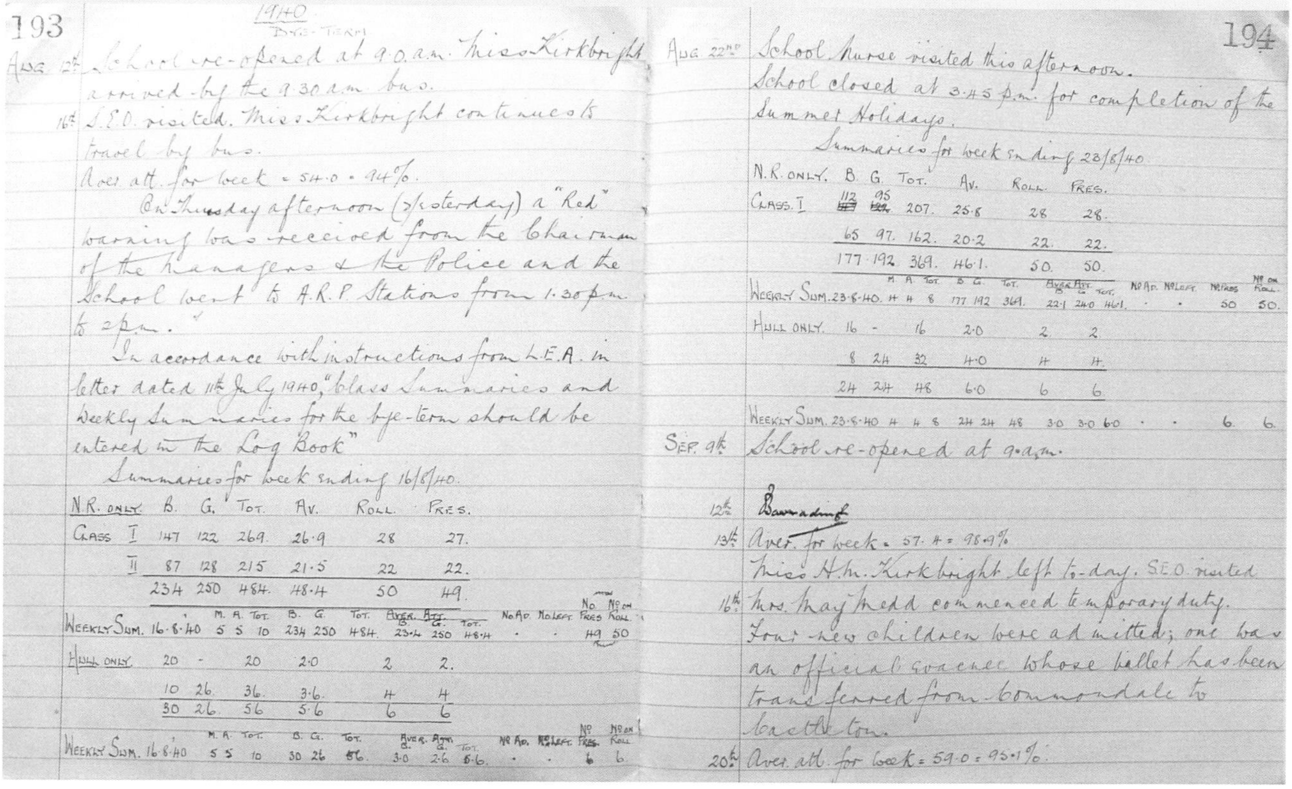

193

1940
Bye-Term

Aug 12th School re-opened at 9.0 a.m. Miss Kirkbright arrived by the 9.30 a.m. bus.
16th S.E.O. visited. Miss Kirkbright continues to travel by bus.
Aver att. for week = 54.0 = 94%.
On Thursday afternoon (yesterday) a "Red" warning was received from the Chairman of the Managers & the Police and the School went to A.R.P. Stations from 1.30 p.m. to 2 p.m.
In accordance with instructions from L.E.A. in letter dated 11th July 1940, "Class Summaries and Weekly Summaries for the bye-term should be entered in the Log Book"
Summaries for week ending 16/8/40.

N.R. only	B.	G.	Tot.	Av.	Roll.	Pres.
Class I	147	122	269.	26·9	28	27.
II	87	128	215	21·5	22	22.
	234	250	484.	48·4	50	49.

Weekly Sum. 16·8·40 M. 5 A. 5 Tot. 10 B. 234 G. 250 Tot. 484. Aver. Att. B. 23·4 G. 250 Tot. 48·4 No Ad. · No Left · No Pres 49 No on Roll 50

Hull only	B.	G.	Tot.	Av.	Roll.	Pres.
	20	-	20	2·0	2	2.
	10	26.	36.	3·6.	4	4
	30	26.	56	5·6	6	6

Weekly Sum. 16·8·40 M. 5 A. 5 Tot. 10 B. 30 G. 26 Tot. 56. Aver. Att. B. 3·0 G. 2·6 Tot. 5·6. No Ad. · No Left · No Pres. 6 No on Roll 6.

194

Aug 22nd School Nurse visited this afternoon.
School closed at 3.45 p.m. for completion of the Summer Holidays.
Summaries for week ending 28/8/40

N.R. only.	B.	G.	Tot.	Av.	Roll.	Pres.
Class I	112	95	207.	25·8	28	28.
	65	97.	162.	20·2	22.	22.
	177	192	369.	46·1.	50.	50.

Weekly Sum. 23·8·40. M. 4 A. 4 Tot. 8 B. 177 G. 192 Tot. 369. Aver. Att. B. 22·1 G. 24·0 Tot. 46·1. No Ad. · No Left · No Pres 50 No on Roll 50.

Hull only.	B.	G.	Tot.	Av.	Roll.	Pres.
	16	-	16	2·0	2	2
	8	24	32	4·0	4	4.
	24	24	48	6·0	6	6

Weekly Sum. 23·8·40 M. 4 A. 4 Tot. 8 B. 24 G. 24 Tot. 48 Aver. Att. B. 3·0 G. 3·0 Tot. 6·0 No Ad. · No Left · No Pres. 6. No on Roll 6.

Sep. 9th School re-opened at 9 a.m.
12th Barnarding
13th Aver. for week = 57.4 = 95·9%
Miss H. M. Kirkbright left to-day. S.E.O. visited
16th Mrs. May Medd commenced temporary duty.
Four new children were admitted; one was an official evacuee whose billet has been transferred from Commondale to Castleton.
20th Aver. att. for week = 59·0 = 95·1%.

January 10th 1939 *Miss Bannister absent with influenza.*
February 20th 1939 *Head unwell, Miss Bannister in sole charge.*
February 22nd 1939 *Miss Fishpool took charge.*

The head resumed his duties on 13th March.

Nevertheless, Mr Hay did his best to widen the horizons of the children.

June 8th 1939 *School closed at 3.45 p.m. for the School Excursion to London.*

Soon afterwards of course the entries once more take on a sinister note and we learn about the local arrangements as war broke out again.

September 1ˢᵗ 1939 *School closed for lessons under the Government Education Scheme until further notice. Evacuees from Hull expected.*
September 7ᵗʰ 1939 *School reopened for the Hull evacuees under their own teacher. 12 children.*
September 19ᵗʰ 1939 *School reopened for normal registration and instruction for the North Riding Children and the evacuees.*

Schools were instructed by the Local Education Authority to keep summaries of class attendance. These were duly entered in the log book (Fig. 3.7).

In spite of the national difficulties of being at war, school life seems to have continued much as before although it cannot have been easy to run two schools within the same building. The last of the evacuees left the school on July 30ᵗʰ 1943.

Inevitably, there were some shortages and provision was made in the event of enemy attack.

March 12ᵗʰ 1940 *School ran out of coke, only 43 °F (6 °C) in school.*
May 24ᵗʰ 1940 *Sand obtained, hope to get bags or boxes to make the cellar "bomb proof".*

Occasionally the war seems to have come too close for comfort and its realities became part of everyday life.

July 3ʳᵈ 1940 *Air raid warning, planes heard but no bombs.*
February 11ᵗʰ 1941 *Gas masks checked and tested.*
November 19ᵗʰ 1942 *This evening at 4.30 p.m. an army tank skidded and smashed down the double gates of the school demolishing the two pillars and about six feet of the boundary wall. Later three other tanks damaged the wall of the school and School House in three different places.*

The gate posts were later replaced with brick (Fig. 3.8).

October 9ᵗʰ 1942 *Children collected 3st of rosehips to be sent to factories for syrup.*
September 24ᵗʰ 1943 *5st of hips sent.*
July 21ˢᵗ 1944 *Dr Butler from London called to thank the children for the collection of rosehips and fox glove seeds.*

Rose hip syrup is rich in Vitamin C and foxglove seeds yield the drug *Digitalis* used to steady heart rate and to treat internal haemorrhaging. Castleton School appears, therefore, to have had a small part to play in the war effort.

Moreover, even in the midst of war, there were some improvements within the school.

January 7ᵗʰ 1941 *Electric light being installed in school.*
January 15ᵗʰ 1941 *Electric light used for the first time.*
May 2ⁿᵈ 1941 *Cups, saucers, plates and one water jug received, plus a stirrup pump.*
December 4ᵗʰ 1944 *School canteen completed and a cook appointed.*
December 14ᵗʰ 1944 *Canteen opened, 27 stayed to dinner.*

And so began the era of liver and onions, fish-on-Fridays, tapioca and roly-poly pudding. Having meals cooked on the premises sometimes had unexpected benefits too.

February 9ᵗʰ 1945 *Repairs to roof. Three workmen stayed to dinner.*

In October 1939 it was recorded that the school was to procure land *AT ONCE* for a school garden, presumably part of the Dig for Victory initiative. In March 1943 the land was measured up and on April 9ᵗʰ the head master recorded that the children were in the garden for the first time. This was the land that is now occupied by the infants' classroom. Unfortunately, it seems to have proved to be yet more work for the head master.

Fig. 3.8 Large gateway with post-war brick gateposts.

July 14ᵗʰ 1944 *Head teacher able to get into the garden for some much needed attention to weeds.*

And with a sigh of relief:

September 19ᵗʰ 1941 *New furnace arrived in sections.*

But the old familiar story continued.

January 23ʳᵈ 1942 *School very cold in spite of the new furnace. Less than 50°F (10°C).*

At long last there is an entry in red ink in the log book:

May 8ᵗʰ 1945 *VICTORY DAY. School closed for two days.*

And again in red ink:

August 30ᵗʰ 1945 *Peace proclaimed with surrender of Japan on 14ᵗʰ August. Three days added to the summer holidays to commemorate this.*

At least one returning soldier was invited into school to add to the children's education.

February 13ᵗʰ 1946 *Mr Mead, formerly a scholar at the school, gave a talk on Palestine where he had been stationed.*

Inevitably, the declaration of peace notwithstanding, the heating system continued to give trouble and the winter of 1947 proved to be one of the coldest on record.

February 4ᵗʰ 1947 *Severe snow, only 22 out of 43 children present.*
February 19ᵗʰ 1947 *Furnace refuses to draw. THERE IS NO OTHER MEANS OF HEATING THE ROOM. Less than 50°F (10°C).*
February 26ᵗʰ 1947 *Blizzard conditions. Only 6 children arrived. We are now cut off by road and rail from the outside world.*

It was another two months before the head master recorded:

March 24ᵗʰ 1947 *Snow began to thaw.*

In common with all other schools in the country, Castleton School had extra holiday days for the marriage of Princess Elizabeth and Prince Philip (November 19ᵗʰ 1947) and then for the celebration of the silver wedding of the King George VI and Queen Elizabeth (April 26ᵗʰ 1948).

The school was also to be affected by another local event because on May 31ˢᵗ 1948, Commondale School closed and 10 children were transferred to Castleton (Fig. 3.9).

By the following year the handwriting in the log book is beginning to deteriorate and occasionally others make the entries. One or two of these suggest that Mr Hay had kept a close eye on supplies. Mrs Swift writes:

July 13ᵗʰ 1949 *New pens, pencils and rubbers were today issued from the stock cupboard. Paint brushes were also requested for the infant class. Good work cannot be accomplished with "inferior tools" and as the stock*

Fig. 3.9 Page from the managers' minute book, 1948.

... Hall Fund function.
Heating appar. — It was reported that the heating apparatus at Castleton had worked satisfactorily since the previous meeting.
Commondale School closure. — The Managers suggestion for the closing of Commondale School had been considered by the Education Committee, and it had been resolved to cease to maintain the school. A copy of the notice published had been forwarded for the information of the managers.
It was proposed to discontinue the school after May 31st and transfer the children to Castleton School. Travelling arrangements were, morning journey per 8.33am train from Commondale, and return by special road transport.
Report. — A copy of a further report on Commondale School, dated Nov. 4th 1947, was submitted to the managers.
Caretaker. — The Commondale caretaker had asked to be relieved of her duties as from March 31st, and it was suggested that Mrs J Foster would undertake the duties.
The Managers were agreeable to this and the Correspondent was instructed to write Northallerton accordingly.
This concluded the business of the meeting.

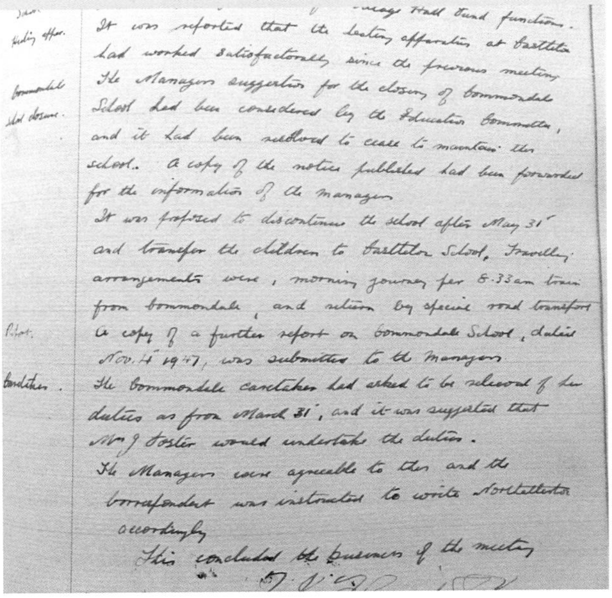

was sufficient to meet this need it was felt that such action was justified. The materials today distributed are being collected at the end of each day.
July 27th 1949 *Cupboards and drawers have today been thoroughly cleaned out in preparation for the mid-summer holidays and it was found necessary to take a new duster out of the stock cupboard.*

On August 30th Mr Hay returned to school after an absence of three months. He had a heart problem and by November 1949 was occasionally having to return to the school house even during lesson time. By December his handwriting had deteriorated even further but it was proving difficult to find a replacement for him.

December 22nd 1949 *I learn that Miss Turner who was offered the post of Head Mistress of the school as my successor has turned it down owing to the unsatisfactory state of the School House. Her parents, whom she had hoped would come to reside with her, found the house far too damp.*

In the opening months of 1950 Mr Hay was becoming increasingly unwell. The school had to be closed occasionally owing to his ill health. He agreed to continue as best he could as there had been no new appointment. However, in April of that year Mr Ronald Reed was appointed to the position and would take up his post after the Easter holiday. Mr Hay retired after 24 years and 3 months at the school (Fig. 3.10). The managers' minute book tells us that he was given a shooting stick as a retirement gift and that it was put on show in the Post Office window so that all the villagers could see it. It is to be hoped that Mr Hay was able to enjoy his retirement, in spite of his ill health, after so many years' service to the school.

Fig. 3.10 Mr Hay's final entry in the log book.

Miss B. Mason, on leave from her Training College has very kindly assisted me for the greater part of this week. School closed at 3.45 p.m. for Easter Holiday.
I take my final leave of the School to-day after twenty four years and three months' service.
Chas. L. Hay 16/2/53.

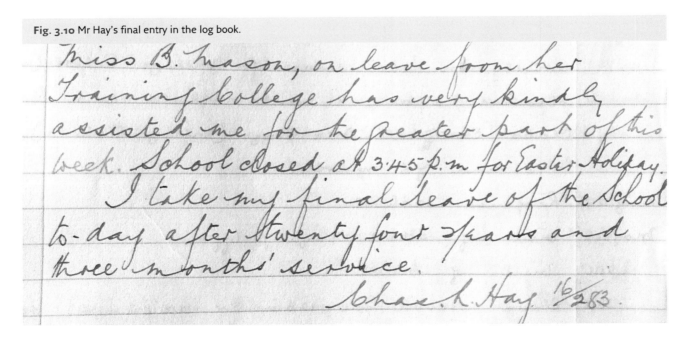

NOTES

1 This name has two different spellings in the log book record.

Post-War Reading Schemes

THE LATE 1940s saw national changes within our education service following the passing of the 1944 Education Act. Prior to this, most children had been educated in a single elementary school. However, schools were now to be divided into primary and secondary education, although it was several years before the 11 – 13 year olds were transferred from Castleton. The Act made education compulsory for children aged 5 – 15, provided for free school milk for all children and introduced the 11+ examination.

Figs. 3.11–3.13 Pages from the Janet and John first reader *Here We Go*.

Come, John, come.

Look, John, look.

Come, little dog.
Come.
Come and look.

Janet, Janet.
Come and look.
See the little dog.

See the kitten.
Come and see.
See the kitten, Janet.
One little kitten.

I see two kittens
Look, John.
See the two kitt
Look down here

Alongside these changes there was a concerted effort to raise standards of literacy. Two reading schemes, Beacon and Happy Venture Readers, were developed during the war and immediate post-war years and were used widely throughout schools in England. It is easy to be critical of these today and view them as stereotyped and sexist as well as being middle class. Nevertheless, many children learned to read with these books, myself included. Happy Venture readers would go on to be used in school for at least thirty years, were revised in 1971 and were still in use when I was first teaching in the mid-1970s. Dick and Dora with their pets Fluff and Nip of the Happy Venture Readers and Janet and John of the Beacon Reader books became keys to the world of words for several generations of school pupils. The Janet and John books were used at Castleton School (Figs. 3.11 – 3.16).

Figs. 3.14-3.16 Pages from the Janet and John early reader *Off to Play*.

This is Janet.

This is John.

This is Mother.

This is Father.

Run, little dog, run.
Look at the little dog.
The little dog can run fast.

The little dog can jump.
Jump, little dog, jump.
Mother, look at my little dog

The 1950s, 60s and 70s

ONE OF THE FIRST issues that Mr Reed had to deal with was once again not directly related to the education of the children but was something that had arisen earlier. Many people will remember the mid-morning milk served in third-of-a-pint bottles, introduced, as we have seen, after 1944.

From the managers' minute book:

> July 14th 1949 *Mr Macdonald* (one of the managers) *reported that the children at Castleton appeared to be drinking the mid-morning milk out of the bottles instead of through straws and thought this was rather unsatisfactory. The correspondent was asked to see Mr Hay about this in case it was an oversight on his part.*
> January 25th 1950 *The correspondent reports of having been informed by the head teacher that straws were obtained locally but supplies had not been available at that time. As the position was improved it was decided to await the arrival of the new head teacher before further action.*
> October 13th 1950 *The question of the milk straws was being dealt with and would be provided by the milk supplier.*
> February 20th 1951 *Still no milk straws.*

However, it was to get worse.

> January 6th 1953 *No school milk is being supplied to the school. Mr Knaggs has informed the Food Office that he can no longer deliver same and up to the present no person willing to do so has been found.*

These and other records make it clear that schools were often having to deal with practical issues far removed from education, added to which there was often a long delay in getting anything done as all major issues had to be dealt with via County Hall at Northallerton.

The old familiar story continues. Again from the managers' minute book:

> June 18th 1954 *Mr Reed requested of the managers that the heating apparatus be attended to before winter.*
> September 28th 1955 *Heating will not be attended to, a letter of protest is to be sent to Northallerton.*
> November 29th 1956 *Managers are to request Northallerton to put the boiler into a satisfactory condition and ask for hot water to be installed.*
> November 20th 1957 *Mr Reed reported an improvement in the heating but there is no reply regarding the hot water.*
> October 10th 1958 *A letter from Northallerton says that a hot water system for Castleton School is to be considered in the next programme of Capital Expenditure.*
> March 11th 1959 *Tenders are invited regarding the installation of a hot water system.*

The hot water system was fitted in June 1959. This matter alone shows just how long it took to get anything done to improve conditions at the school.

The log books continue to provide evidence of our social history as well as the history of the school. For instance, the first entry in ball point pen rather than pen and ink was made in June 1951. Other, more important, national issues are also recorded.

June 7th 1951 *School closed this day so that Mr Reed, Miss Mason and 9 children could go to London with the Cleveland School Excursion to the Festival of Britain Exhibition.*

December 15th 1951 *A Poplar tree planted, given to the school in connection with the Festival of Britain activities.*

February 15th 1952 *Funeral of George VI. Two minutes silence. Juniors and seniors attended a service in the parish church.*

October 22nd 1952 *A Manager has been appointed to represent Castleton at a public meeting to consider the Coronation Celebrations.*

April 21st 1953 *Received notice that after the Midsummer Holidays the school would become a Primary School and the Seniors would go to the new Eskdale School at Whitby.*

Since 1874 the children had stayed at Castleton firstly until they were twelve and then thirteen or fourteen.

Of course more local matters also continue to be recorded.

January 29th 1953 *Two oil stoves delivered.*

February 2nd 1953 *Severe gales over the weekend. Gap in the school roof, majority of slates on the north side of the house blown off.*

July 8th 1953 *5 tons 12 cwt 1 qr of coke delivered.*

At the end of the summer term 1953, Westerdale School closed and once again Castleton took the children from another village school.

September 7th 1953 *Number on roll 53, 5 children transferred from Westerdale.*

At last conditions within the school seem to have been improving, or were they?

January 7th 1954 *During the holidays half of the school roof was stripped and retiled. Beading placed around classrooms to stop draughts. Partition near the furnace was put further back and covered with asbestos.*[1]

For some time the matter of radiators being fitted in the school had been discussed at length.

October 14th 1955 *Five radiators installed over the half term holiday.*

The school was now warmer and, following the introduction of the National Health Service in 1948, there were other improvements for the children: their teeth were given more attention and vaccination programmes were introduced. Throughout the 1950s there are records of regular visits of the school dentist including many records of the extraction of teeth and in October 1959 there is a record of the children being given injections against polio.

A group of Castleton school girls was photographed towards the close of this decade (Fig. 4.1). At that time there were three members of the Flintoft family in one class: two sisters and their cousin.

The 1960s saw several national school closures for various events. On May 6th 1960 school was closed for the wedding of Princess Margaret to Anthony Armstrong-Jones and on June 8th 1961 for the wedding of the Duke of Kent to Katherine Worsley, from Hovingham Hall (Fig. 4.2). On June 25th 1965 the school was closed once again, this time to celebrate the 700th anniversary of Simon de Montfort's Parliament and the 750th anniversary of the signing of Magna Carta.

There is a snap shot from the early 1960s (Fig. 4.3).

Familiar local names continue to make an appearance:

January 11th 1963 *Admitted Margaret Baxter from Danby.*

April 20th 1963 *Elsie Mould appointed cleaner at the school.*

Fig. 4.1 A group of Castleton School girls in 1959.
Back row – Susan Kitching, Linda Stonehouse, Shirley Williamson, Barbara MacDonald, unknown, Mary Gill?, Carolyne Stanforth.
Front row – Valerie Dowson, Valerie Williamson, Janet Flintoft, Carol Milner, Pat Thompson, Daphne Flintoft.

Fig. 4.2 Log book record of the school holiday for the wedding of the Duke and Duchess of Kent, June 8th 1961.

> June 8th. School closed – Wedding at York Minster of H. R. H. The Duke of Kent and Miss Katharine Worsley of Hovingham, the daughter of the Lord Lieutenant of the North Riding.

Fig. 4.3 A photograph from the early 1960s.
Back row – Philip Stonehouse, Alan Mould, Sheila Flintoft, Linda Muir, face not showing, David Dowson, Stuart Thompson, Andrew Cornforth.
Middle row – Eileen Booth (with hair bow), unknown, Carol Flintoft, Ruth Iredale, Jennifer Cockerill, Richard Bell.
Front row – Robert Hartley (known as the Milky Bar Kid), Chris Flintoft, Ian Rossiter, Kathleen Willis, Kenneth Mason.

Horizons were widening as Mr Reed seems to have taken the children out of school each summer.

July 1955 *School excursion to Barnard Castle and Teesdale.*

August 2nd 1957 *Excursion to Lake Ullswater.*

July 15th 1965 *Two buses to the Yorkshire Show.*

July 8th 1966 *Two buses to Barnard Castle, Bowes Museum and High Force.*

Fig. 4.4 Mr Reed's retirement, July 1966.
Back row left to right – Mrs O Hutchinson (manager), Mr H Oddy (organiser), Mrs N Macdonald (chairman of managers), Miss Beryl Mason (infant teacher), Ruth Iredale, Richard Bell. Front row left to right – Mr R Reed, Mrs Reed, Bridget Champion, Andrew Cornforth.

Fig. 4.5 Log book record of three classes, September 1966.

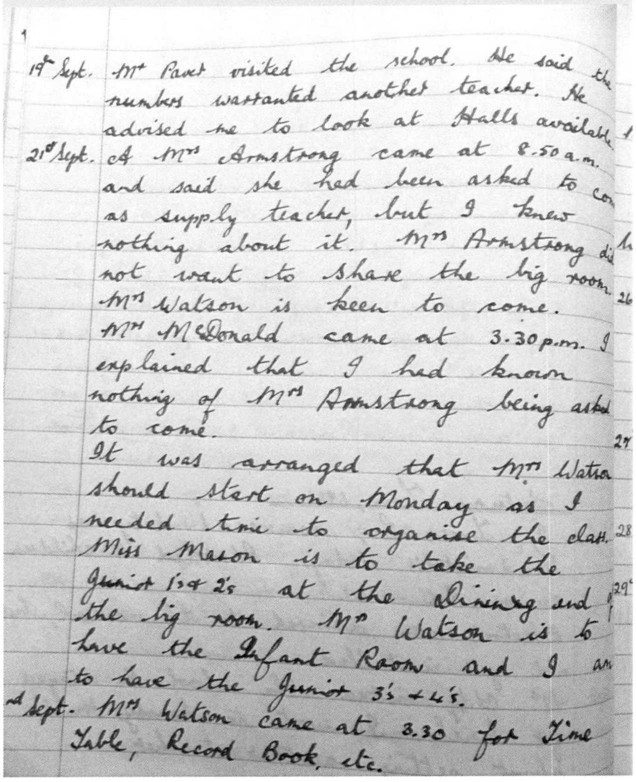

19th Sept. Mr Pout visited the school. He said the numbers warranted another teacher. He advised me to look at Halls available. 21st Sept. A Mrs Armstrong came at 8.50 a.m. and said she had been asked to come as supply teacher, but I knew nothing about it. Mrs Armstrong did not want to share the big room. Mrs Watson is keen to come. Mrs McDonald came at 3.30 p.m. I explained that I had known nothing of Mrs Armstrong being asked to come. It was arranged that Mrs Watson should start on Monday as I needed time to organise the class. Miss Mason is to take the Junior 1s & 2s at the dining end of the big room. Mrs Watson is to have the Infant Room and I am to have the Junior 3s & 4s. Sept. Mrs Watson came at 3.30 for Time Table, Record Book, etc.

Fig. 4.6 Main classroom showing the new partition.
Photograph taken after 1968.

Throughout his years at the school, Mr Reed introduced a library and also oversaw considerable improvements to the school building. As well as the installation of the hot water system, the roof was retiled and all of the timber was treated for woodworm. It was also during Mr Reed's headship that schools generally began to enter the age of technology with a gramophone arriving in 1953 and a new radio installed in 1957.

At the end of the summer term 1966, Mr Reed retired after 16 years at the school (Fig. 4.4). Miss Teresa Loo was appointed head mistress, taking up her post in the September term. Miss Loo was to teach the upper juniors, Miss Mason had the lower juniors while Mrs Watson taught the infants (Fig. 4.5).

Like all newly appointed head teachers, Miss Loo wanted to develop the school and straight away she took up the call for improvements to be made. On September 29th she asked for a telephone to be put in and on October 28th a cooker, electric potato peeler and a wall heater were installed in the kitchen. Just a month later there is another particularly interesting entry regarding the kitchen.

> November 11th 1966 *Miss Campbell, the catering supervisor, complimented Mrs Armstrong on the cleanliness of the pans and other equipment in the kitchen, in use for over 20 years.*

The telephone was installed the following year.

> November 28th 1967 *Telephone installed. The number is Castleton 496.*

And during the first Christmas holiday of Miss Loo's headship, painters started to decorate the school, although she does make the remark *It is to be painted in the same colours!* A month later a new library unit was delivered to the school and the following December work began on building a partition across the large classroom. However, this had taken some time to come about.

> June 21st 1967 *Mr Adkin* (the building inspector) *came to measure the big classroom with a view to erecting a partition across it to make two classrooms. He was estimating the cost.*
> September 5th 1967 *Nothing has been done about the partition.*
> September 26th 1967 *Mr Adkin came to say that work on the partition was being put out to tender.*
> December 21st 1967 *Mr Berwick came, when school closed, to start work on the Partition across the big room.*
> January 8th 1968 *The Partition was not completed during the holidays because the track has not arrived. Back to the curtain!*
> February 26th 1968 *School reopened after the holiday. Work on the Partition was completed by Wednesday. We are very pleased with it.* (Fig. 4.6)

This partition would be replaced with a breeze block wall with a linking door in the 1990s and removed altogether in the early years of this century. There is now a folding, sound-proof partition in place, which can be opened or closed as needed.

Other improvements went on too.

> November 4th 1968 *During the holidays the boys' toilets were covered in. Stone from Fryup was used to blend in with the existing building – an excellent job.*
> January 29th 1969 *A spirit duplicator was bought second hand from Boosbeck School.*

These were also known as Banda machines. Banda machines were invented in 1923 and used throughout schools in the USA and the UK until the late 1970s, being phased out with the introduction of the first photocopiers. Many of us will remember standing beside the Banda machine, turning the handle to churn out copies of work for the children. Those were the days, fingers stained with purple ink!

Miss Loo also oversaw the introduction of the television to the school as well as a record player.

Fig. 4.7 The infants' classroom in the 1990s.

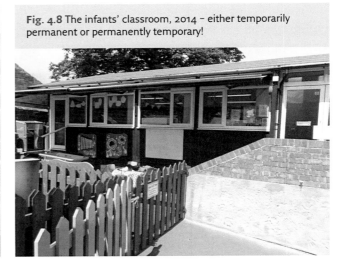

Fig. 4.8 The infants' classroom, 2014 – either temporarily permanent or permanently temporary!

December 18th 1968 *A Christmas Concert was held in School at 2 p.m. A very good audience. Collection taken for school fund amounted to £6. The parents saw the Record Player which we had bought out of School Fund. Everyone was very pleased.*

October 13th 1970 *TV arrived but no aerial!*

There is an amusing entry in the manager's minute book during that year:

June 9th 1970 *Toilet facilities in all old schools are being looked into by the Education Authority.*

In January 1970, Miss Loo asked for more storage within school and the idea of making a stock cupboard in the main classroom was suggested. As yet another example of how long work took at that time: it was 1978, after Miss Loo had left the school, before the stock cupboard was installed.

However, a major improvement was made that is still in use today. In July 1970, Mr Potts, the county architect, came to the school regarding a temporary classroom. In September workmen came to measure the playground for this. There is a detailed record of the arrival of the (very permanent) 'temporary' classroom. It stands where the school garden used to be.

September 11th 1970 *Tarren's men started building brick pillars for the temporary classroom.*

September 23rd 1970 *Men arrived to start erecting the classroom.*

November 2nd 1970 *Painters started in the new room.*

November 10th 1970 *Painters finished, heaters delivered.*

November 11th 1970 *Lino laid. Room ready for electricians.*

The linoleum was to do service for over twenty years, replaced by carpet in 1994.

November 20th 1970 *Mr Paver* (role not recorded but probably a building contractor) *called. I had already made a number of calls about the electricians not coming.*

November 21st and 22nd 1970 *Saturday and Sunday, electricians at work.*

November 23rd 1970 *Room ready at last. Furniture and books moved across, Miss Mason's class to start on Tuesday.* (Figs. 4.7 & 4.8)

Summer trips continued with a visit to Fountains Abbey, Harrogate and Knaresborough in July 1967, to the Great Yorkshire Show in July 1969 and to the Lake District in July 1970. Concerts were also held in the playground during the early 1970s as there was not enough room in school for children and parents together (Figs. 4.9, 4.10 & 4.11).

Professional school photographs were by this time taken annually. However, as more people now had cameras (the Kodak Instamatic was introduced in 1963) and photography was becoming a much cheaper hobby there are many more photographs from this period. They record changing fashions, the introduction of colour film and, above all, they provide us with a window onto life at Castleton School (Figs. 4.12 – 4.23).

By the early 1970s discussions began to take place regarding changes at Castleton following the introduction of Primary Area Planning.

May 17th 1972 *Public meeting held to discuss proposals for a new Castleton County School contained in the Draft Plan for Primary Schools.*
October 13th 1972 *Meeting regarding the draft plan addressed by Mr Macklin and Lord Swinton.*
September 1973 *Final draft plan.*
October 19th 1973 *Mr Winter and Earl of Swinton visited the school.*

Fig. 4.9 Mrs Connie Watson on the front playground with children practising for a concert.

Fig. 4.10 Miss Loo with recorder group.

Fig. 4.11 Miss Loo leading the recorder group at an outdoor concert on the back playground.

Fig. 4.12 School photograph, 1968. On the left Miss Beryl Mason, on the right Miss Teresa Loo and Mrs Connie Watson.

Fig. 4.13 Five little girls from Westerdale sitting on the front step enjoying the sunshine.
Left to right – Caroline Muir, Marian Mortimer, Janet Dowey, Cath Flintoft, Jenny Willis.
Note the Victorian boot scraper to the right of the step. This was removed in the early 1980s when the playground was resurfaced.

Fig. 4.14 Mrs Connie Watson with her class, 1967.

Fig. 4.15 Mrs Connie Watson with her class, 1967.

Fig. 4.16 Miss Beryl Mason with her class, 1967.

Fig. 4.17 Miss Teresa Loo with her class, 1967.

Fig. 4.18 The school football team early 1970s. Note the roof of the 'temporary' classroom on the left and the wire fencing on the right.

Fig. 4.19 Miss Loo, Mrs Watson and Miss Mason with the whole school, 1972 or '73.

Fig. 4.20 The lower junior classroom *circa* 1970.

Fig. 4.21 The lower junior classroom *circa* 1970.

Fig. 4.22 Miss Beryl Mason with her class before November 1970.

Fig. 4.23 School photograph summer 1971.
Back row – Mrs Connie Watson, Adrienne Taylor, Keith Dowey, Stephen Cook, Andrew Lillie, Phillip Wilkinson, Mark Watson, Raymond Flintoft, Fiona McCaskie, Richard Trousdale, Susan Smith, Sharon Taylor, Judith Muir, Rowena Smith, Colin Grice, Miss Teresa Loo, Miss Beryl Mason
Third row – Ann Moss, Paul Thompson, Marian Mortimer, Nicholas Longstaff, Jane Surtees, Ian Martin, Catherine Flintoft, Graeme Thompson, Gillian Cook, Ruth Cooper, Mark Trees, Terence Booth, Elaine Gray
Second row – Tina Harding, Karen Gray, Stuart Champion, Alison Muir, Susan Thompson, Rebecca Trees, Sandra Flintoft, Bridget Champion, Catherine Longstaff, Sally Watson, Andrew Muir, Katy Champion, Russell Watson, Andrew Williamson, Melanie Harding
Front row – Stuart Lillie, Jackie Champion, Gordon Booth, Steven Thompson, Jackie Grice, Charles Balding, Christopher Martin, Jane Stephenson, Adam Pacey, Christopher Smith, William Wells, Ian Robbins, Christopher Gray, Kevin Williamson

The issue of a new school would continue to be raised both in the early 1990s and once again in 2000. However, these plans were not to come to fruition and, sadly, Miss Loo's time at the school was to be foreshortened due to her ill health. In September 1974, Mr Ross took on the role of acting head and was to oversee the centenary celebrations of the school.

Just four years before the actual anniversary, however, the school had taken part in Education Week. Miss Loo made a particularly interesting entry in the log book.

May 7th 1970 *As part of our Education Week Activities we held a Parents' Evening in School. It was very well attended and we had a most enjoyable evening. Some of the parents have lived here all their lives and found the first Log Book of 1874 very interesting. They could trace the families of the first pupils of the School. One of them still lives in the Village and is 101 years old (Mrs Alexander) and can remember being a Monitor when the School first opened.*

To commemorate the centenary the children and staff dressed up in Victorian costume and a photograph of the whole school was taken to mark the occasion, which was held on October 18th 1974 (Fig. 4.24). The children were given a real taste of what school life was like in Victorian times (Fig. 4.25). There was a centenary programme for the day (Figs. 4.26 & 4.27). The event was duly recorded and the resulting film shown in school.

November 20th 1974 *Parents evening – tremendous success – school bulging at the seams. Two slide shows by the Vicar and an audio-video tape of the happenings on the Centenary day shown by Mr Simpson.*

Centenary or not, the state of the heating continued to be a problem.

April 9th 1975 *Mr Johnson, heating engineer, called regarding inadequate heating of the school and fumes entering the main classroom. He agreed that the heating was inadequate and that fumes from the boiler were entering the classroom.*

Fig. 4.24 School photograph taken for the centenary, 1974.

Fig. 4.25 Mrs Connie Watson keeping order in her (very small) Victorian class. Note the west boundary wall before the buttresses.

Fig. 4.26 Drawing of the front of the school by E M Plummer.

Fig. 4.27 Front cover of the Centenary Programme using E M Plummer's drawing, 1974.

Castleton School Centenary

1874 November 1974

October half term 1975 *An oil fired boiler installed.*

February half term 1976 *New ceiling fitted.*

In September 1976 Miss Loo announced her intention to retire and a presentation was made to her on December 21st. Mr Ross continued as temporary head teacher.

The following year was the Queen's Silver Jubilee. The whole of Castleton joined in a three-day celebration to mark the occasion (Fig. 4.28).

July 14th 1977 *The whole school went to Grangetown to see the Queen. All saw the Queen at close range.*

The children also saw HMS *Britannia* and the school was given a jubilee plaque.

On July 22nd Mr Ross ended his 'temporary' appointment *after three very enjoyable years.*

In September 1977, Mr Stan Moore took up his post as the new head. Once again the log book records improvements to the fabric of the school.

Fig. 4.28 Programme of events for the Silver Jubilee, June 1977.

PROGRAMME OF EVENTS

Sunday, 5th June, 11 a.m.
Castleton Church. Silver Jubilee Service.
A United Act of Thanksgiving.
The Royal British Legion will be present.

Monday, 6th June, 3 p.m. - 5 p.m.
Treasure Hunt.
Start—British Legion Hall.

Tuesday, 7th June.
11 a.m.—Judging of Contest for :
Best decorated house
Best decorated business premises.

1-30 p.m.—Grand Fancy Dress Parade
Led by British Legion
Assemble at Castleton School.
Route :—High Street through Castle Close returning to Downe Arms Field.

2-00 p.m.—Sports on Downe Arms Field.
1. Cross Country Race 12+ handicapped (Trophy)
2. Flat Race Under 5yrs.
3. Flat Race 5-7yrs.
4. Balloon Bursting Race Ladies
5. Flat Race 8-11yrs.
6. 3 Legged Race 5-11yrs. handicapped.
7. Egg and Spoon Race Ladies
8. Obstacle Race 9-12yrs.
9. Needle Threading Race Men
10. Wheel-barrow Race 12-16yrs.
11. Slow Cycle Race Open handicapped
12. Wheel-barrow Race 9-12yrs.
13. Sack Race Open handicapped
14. Obstacle Race 12-16yrs.
15. Flat Race 11+
16. Tug-of-War. Teams to be made up of residents of Castleton. Crate of beer & trophy for winning team.

Welly Throwing Competition Open
Continuous from 2-15 p.m.
Trophy for winning competitor.

Bale Throwing Competition Men
Continuous from 2-15 p.m.

Presentation of prizes after each event by Miss T. Loo.

4-00 — 6-00 p.m.
Tea in Temperance Hall.
Draw for Raffle.

Presentation of Crown Pieces by Miss T. Loo.

8-00 p.m.—Domino Drive in Temperance Hall.

8-00 — 11 p.m.
Disco-Barbecue in Downe Arms Field.

GOD SAVE THE QUEEN

October half term 1977 *Dining room floor sanded and sealed.*

October 17th 1977 *Began discussions regarding an inside toilet.*

November 11th 1977 *Wrote to County Hall regarding the urgent need for a stock room.*

March 3rd 1978 *Contractors came to measure up for a toilet and a stock room.*

May 5th 1978 *Wrote to County Hall about the possibility of a porch for the girls' toilet.*

June half term 1978 *Stock room and staff toilet fitted but toilet walls not sound proof so will have to be replaced.*

March 30th 1979 *Outside PE store completed.*

Outings to other places continued to be a part of school life for the children, including a trip to the Lake District in 1970, and with a residential visit becoming an important aspect of the annual programme. There were two trips in the closing year of the 1970s.

March 4th 1979 *Thirty-five children and six adults went to London. Visited Madame Tussaud's, The Royal Academy Gold of El Dorado Exhibition and had a coach tour. Returned by train.*

October 8th 1979 *Twenty upper juniors with Egton and Grosmont Schools for a week at Ingleborough Hall Outdoor Education Centre.*

NOTES

1   At that time the dangers of asbestos were not known. The partition was replaced with a non-asbestos compound in 1984.

The 1980s and 1990s

M R STAN MOORE left the school in July 1981 and Mr Nigel Snow came as acting head for one term. At the close of his time at the school, Mr Snow wrote:

December 18ᵗʰ 1981 *Term ended, so did my term at Castleton, which was one of the most enjoyable terms I have ever spent in teaching.*

In January 1982, Mr Dave Chapman took up his post as head teacher of the school. He arrived in the middle of a particularly cold winter and, in order to keep up the tradition, he soon had to contend with a cold school.

January 11ᵗʰ 1982 *Water pipes frozen, toilets OK so stumbled through the day. General temperature fell uncomfortably. After school I tried to contact a plumber with little luck – with prospect of another cold night I was forced to declare school closed until further notice. What a start!*

Fig. 5.1 Miss Beryl Mason with the whole school, March 1983. Note the wooden floor boards; carpet was first fitted in 1994.

Alongside coping with the cold, Mr Chapman also soon faced the prospect of losing a member of staff. In spite of a valiant endeavour to keep the children in three classes, Miss Beryl Mason, who taught the lower juniors, was to be redeployed although she subsequently chose to take early retirement at the end of the spring term 1983.

March 23rd 1983 This evening we said goodbye to Beryl Mason after 38 years loyal service to the school. In excess of 160 people came to the Village Hall where we saw slides of the school's history, the children sang and read poetry. Messers Lilly and Harrison said their farewells for the managers and the education dept.

Fig. 5.2 The whole school with Miss Mason at the piano. Mr Chapman back left, Mrs Watson back right.

Fig. 5.3 School photograph, July 1983. Adults in the centre of the picture, left to right, Mrs Pat Richardson, Mr Dave Chapman, Mrs Connie Watson.

respectively then, after the presentation of a bouquet by Mr D Medd, we spent the rest of the evening over coffee and scones. (Figs. 5.1 & 5.2)

Miss Mason, who was born *circa* 1922, had been a pupil at Castleton and then stayed on as a pupil teacher. She spent most of her life at the school. Her commitment and dedication are here duly acknowledged; she must have taught many children over those years. Miss Mason's death, in April 1987, is recorded in the school log book.

April 25th 1983 *This has been the first full day with 58 children and two teachers.*

Thankfully, this was to change soon afterwards with the arrival of a new family to the district.

June 27th 1983 *Mrs Scarth from Westerdale called in to chat about the children she will be bringing to the school. It is as a result of these children that our numbers have reached the critical 61 and Mrs Richardson's hours are changed to full time for the end of term.*

July 4th 1983 *Today Janine and Adrian Scarth from Westerdale started at the school.* (Fig. 5.3)

Like his predecessors, Mr Chapman was soon making changes at the school.

September 1982 *All juniors in the main building, infants in the temporary classroom.*

At least initially, the lower juniors used the room which is now the office, staff room and storage space while the upper juniors were in the whole of the main classroom. The 'office' was simply a desk at one end of this large classroom where the telephone was also situated (Fig. 5.4). This meant that the head teacher could take the telephone into the staff toilet next door if he needed to take or to make a private call. As Mr Chapman pointed out to me, at least he could deal with calls sitting comfortably!

Fig. 5.4 Upper junior classroom late 1980s. Note the secretary, Mrs Millns, working at the back of the classroom. The purpose-built office was installed in October 1992.

During the autumn term of 1982, evening classes were started at the school providing French, sewing and guitar lessons, the last of which were taken by Mr Chapman. These continued for the following six years.

April 1984 *A photocopier installed.* (This was the end of the era of the Banda machines.)

July 28th 1984 *Mr Millns and I prepared the ground for the plumber to put water into the infant classroom.*

July 29th 1984 *Water plumbed in.*

February 12th 1985 *Held a staff meeting, discussed toilet problem and possible solutions. Unblocked toilets in the morning but were frozen again by 3 p.m.*

February 13th 1985 *School still closed – temperature in toilets did not rise above freezing.*

In January 1987 the school was closed once again on account of frozen toilets. During the winter months attempts were made to prevent the toilets from freezing overnight by placing small paraffin lamps at the side of the basins but, as the records tell us, this didn't always work. In the meantime all of the children had to use the outside toilets while discussions continued regarding the issue of indoor facilities. Eventually the Parent-Teacher Association raised the money and parents did the job of installing toilets in the infant classroom while the school remained in a queue with other rural schools waiting for County Council funding for indoor toilets for the main building.

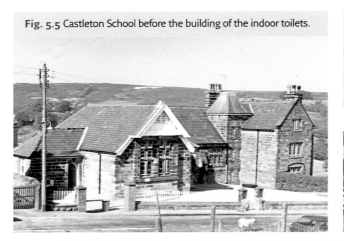

Fig. 5.5 Castleton School before the building of the indoor toilets.

Fig. 5.6 Castleton School after the building of the indoor toilets.

Fig. 5.7 School photograph, summer 1990. Adults left to right – Mrs Maureen Jackson, Mrs Sharon Easton, Mrs Vilna Millns, Mrs Pam Shepherd, Mr Dave Chapman, Mrs Anne Thomas, Mrs Alison Hodgson, Mrs Iris Hutchinson.

Fig. 5.8 Stand of silver birches, July 2014.

January 13th 1987 *Today I had a phone call from the architect in charge of TOILETS. He led me to believe that the junior toilets will be started in March. I am most hopeful.*

It was not until September 1988, however, that the indoor toilets were in use for the first time. A local builder, Newton Builders, was given the contract to install indoor toilets for the junior classes. The builders removed and numbered the stones from in front of the kitchen, built the toilets and then replaced the stones so that it is now impossible to tell that the front of the building has been altered (Figs. 5.5 & 5.6).

September 6th 1988 *The provision of toilets is now complete and all major building work cleared. So starts the first year at the school when all children can go to the toilet in comfort.*

But even these new facilities were to provide their own drama.

September 20th 1989 *Today David Heldt was stuck in the boys toilets – after some real live CDT* (craft, design and technology) *from Mr Wilkinson, the window cleaner, and myself we were able to break David out through the window and after a bit of force work to break the door lock.*

By the late 1980s the administrative aspect of school life was changing. In September 1985, Mrs Vilna Millns was appointed as the school secretary, taking the dinner money and answering the telephone. In the 20 years that Mrs Millns was at the school she saw her role change beyond all recognition. At the end of her term of office she was not only counting dinner money and answering the telephone but was also involved in setting the budget, ordering stock, entering invoices onto the computer as well as filing an ever-growing correspondence.

There were other staff changes too. Mrs Connie Watson retired in December 1987 after more than 21 years at the school. Not long afterwards another, still very familiar, face joined the team at Castleton.

July 14th 1989 *Mrs Shepherd interviewed and appointed.*

Mrs Shepherd took up her post of teaching the Y3/4 children in January 1990 and was to stay at the school for 19 years (Fig. 5.7).

On his arrival, Mr Chapman had wanted to acquire adjoining land for the use of the school. In September 1988, the land on the hillside adjacent to the school was looked at with a view to purchase. By February 1990 work had begun to give access to this garden, which was to be a wildlife area. It has proved to be a very wise purchase indeed.

November 28th 1990 *Today Mr Iredale* (parent) *came into school and brought seven birch trees to plant in the school wildlife area. He showed the children how to plant the trees and then he showed them how he could work on mature trees by climbing the sycamore and taking off a dangerous bough which overhung the infant classroom. The pieces he removed were made into piles in the newly planted area. It is hoped they will rot down and attract insects and birds.*

These piles of wood were still there ten years later and today the silver birches form a stand of mature trees giving shade and providing a habitat for wildlife (Fig. 5.8).

During the 1990s the children kept hens and ducks on this land and in 1996 Mr and Mrs Truscott of Westerdale provided two goats to keep the vegetation under control. The children used the area for a range of lessons, especially science, and held their teddy bears' picnic there in the summer time.

> January 19th 1993 *Today we planted bluebells in the wild area.*
> November 5th 1995 *Paving flags were placed in the school wild area garden. It is hoped this will provide more useable areas of garden for the children's planting.*

A pond was created in the wildlife area in October 1996.

But much bigger changes had been taking place within the classroom. One of the most widespread practical changes was the introduction of computers into primary schools; the first record of a computer at the school is December 1983. The machine was a BBC computer with a tape recorder for loading programmes. Mr Chapman had it at his home for a time while he learnt how to use it and then brought it back to school in his wheelbarrow – a glorious juxtaposition of old and new technologies. The wheelbarrow is still doing sterling service but the computer was out of date within a very short time! (Fig. 5.9)

Changes in Education

MR CHAPMAN began his headship in the days of annual school trips that were whole village outings, half-hour story times at the end of each school day and harvest treats that involved collecting apples from the school orchard by knocking them from the trees, chasing loose ones down the slope and saving the best ones to eat while stretched out on the bank. Those halcyon days have long gone.

Throughout his fifteen and a half years at the school, Mr Chapman's term of office coincided with several local initiatives, such as the Eskdale and the Rural Schools Projects, as well as major changes within the education service of this country as a whole. His headship saw the implementation of the recommendations of the Warnock Report, which led to the Education Act of 1981 and changes to provision for children with special needs. He was in post when the Education Reform Act was passed in 1988, which led to the introduction of the National Curriculum and a national scheme of assessment. In addition staff appraisal and Ofsted inspections were added to the school agenda during those years. On top of that, Mr Chapman also had to oversee an issue that was to have far-reaching implications, especially for small rural primary schools: the introduction of LMS or Local Management of Schools. As we have already seen, it was often difficult to get improvements made to the fabric of the building and even at times difficult to get basic educational supplies when they were needed because everything had to be arranged via County Hall. LMS addressed this issue by giving schools their own delegated budget so that the head teacher, with the agreement of the board of governors, could make local decisions about spending.

Of course all of these changes meant the attendance of many meetings, a great deal of retraining in order to manage those changes and an increase in the amount of paperwork. From a teacher who had some administrative work to do, now the head teacher of a small rural primary school had to become familiar with employment law and recruitment, health and safety legislation as well as building management and budgeting alongside trying to run a school on a day-to-day basis and teach a class. It is to Mr Chapman's credit that he managed the running of the school as well as he did, amidst so many major changes, and that the pupils continued to enjoy their time there and have an enriched childhood as a result.

Fig. 5.9 Computers in the junior classroom, mid-1980s. The infant classroom got its first computer in July 1989.

Music soon became a special feature of the school. For some time the children had been taking part in the Whitby Music Festival; now they were taken to see professional performances as well as local amateur productions. Theatre groups came to the school and the peripatetic music service started to visit on a regular basis. Mr Chapman also began to organise school concerts and shows that have gone down in the annals of local history.

Shows such as *The Snow Queen* (1993), *Bugsy Malone* (1995) and the locally written *Fairy Cross Plain* (1996) and *The Fantastic Toy Shop* (1997) as well as *Joseph and his Amazing Technicolour Dreamcoat* (1998) were put on each year. Some of these were joint productions with Glaisdale School (Figs. 5.10, 5.11 & 5.12). Judging by the log book entry, the Christmas show of 1991, co-produced with Mrs Shepherd, was particularly memorable.

Fig. 5.10 *Fairy Cross Plain* performed at Glaisdale, 1980s.

Fig. 5.11 Some of the cast of *The Fantastic Toy Shop*, 1997. This show was also produced at Castleton in 1988.

Fig. 5.12 Some of the cast of *Joseph and his Amazing Technicolour Dreamcoat*, 1998.

December 12th 1991 *This evening we did the show for the Over 60s. The show was the Christmas Crocodile which readers of this journal will recognise as the very first show I ever put on at this school. I have to say it was a hoot.*

December 13th 1991 *Tonight's performance was stolen by the infant "jugglers" and clowns. The jugglers, being reception children, were perfectly unco-ordinated and the clowns covered everyone with custard pie.*

And it seems that sometimes some of the adults were inspired to take to the stage.

April 23rd 1993 *Today the dinner ladies and canteen staff performed an impromptu and hilarious version of St George and the Dragon. With costumes borrowed from Loftus Sec., including a pantomime horse/dragon, the damsel (Mrs Lillie) was rescued by George (Ellen Boyes) from the jaws of the dragon (Mrs Wedgwood, front – Mrs Hutchinson, back) whilst the storyteller (Mrs Scarth) read the plot. The children cheered and jeered accordingly.*

On another occasion the kitchen staff, known as The Crazy Gang, pulled off a particularly clever stunt. Mr Chapman was called upon to turn plumber and attend to a leak outside. It turned out that it was actually a leek! (Fig. 5.13)

Fig. 5.13 The head teacher taking a spanner to deal with a leaking leek in December 1994. Adults left to right – Mrs Val Lillie, Mrs Iris Hutchinson, Ms Ellen Boyes, Mrs Della Wedgwood, Mrs Pam Scarth and Mr Dave Chapman.

Fig. 5.14 The football team in their smart kit.
Back row – James Thompson, Richard Alderson, David Stonehouse, Lee Nessfield, John Stonehouse.
Front row – Tom Lane, Jack Nightingale, Stuart Dowson, Mark Thompson, John Lillie.

Fig. 5.15 The netball team in theirs.
Back row – Rebecca Muir, Lisa Dale, Lizzie Iredale, Peter Fitton.
Front row – David Stonehouse, Samantha Muir, Lucy Watson, Louise Underwood, Steph Raw.

Sport also began to feature more often in the life of the school including swimming, which had been introduced by Miss Loo, and a popular Sports Day. The children took part in league and friendly football and netball matches as well as joining in small school sports with other schools in the Esk Valley. Parents and friends of the school held a barn dance to raise money for a strip for each of the teams. These were used for several years (Figs. 5.14 & 5.15). The sports events were not without incident and sometimes the results were somewhat disappointing but there was much celebration over successes.

March 11th 1988 *The boys took part in a 5-a-side tournament at Whitby Sports Hall.*

October 7th 1988 *Football at Danby – team somewhat overwhelmed.*

July 19th 1989 *Sports Day was a GREAT success – the weather was so hot we arranged two drinks breaks. The events were all timed team events – The eventual winners being the RED DEVILS.*

November 3rd 1989 *This afternoon the older girls played netball at Danby and the older boys had a football training session – I took the younger boys for football on the sports area. Whilst returning with the girls (victorious girls) my clutch broke but Mr Champion saved the day by taking the teams in the taxi.*

March 17th 1990 *Today we took a team to play at Great Ayton School at football. The entire defence was made up of sixth year girls. It was a smashing day – we did not win but they knew they had played a game, especially their forwards one of whom had to retire hurt!*

April 4th 1992 *The five-a-side team played in a competition at Whitby – they played well winning one match, drawing one and losing two.*

November 5th 1993 *The footballers played a game of football against Glaisdale. It was a very friendly game with a 4-4 result.*

November 20th 1993 *Five-a-side at Whitby Sports Hall – in our mini league we drew two and won one making us equal second in the league.*

November 24th 1995 *This afternoon I took the five-a-side football team to Whitby where they won the small school's shield. They played five games and did not concede a single goal (won 4, drew 1).*

Maypole dancing was also added to the school activities.

May 3rd 1993 *May Day Bank Holiday – the older children performed a May Pole dance for the visitors to the village behind the Downe Arms. This was the culmination of two weeks' rehearsals. It was a great success.*

April 21st 1994 *The school now owns a Maypole and the children were able to dance for real. The pole was made by a parent and is a handsome beast.*

May 2nd 1994 *May Day Bank Holiday. The older children danced around the Maypole as part of the May Day celebrations. The day was fine and the dances successful.*

The children went on to do this for several years and Maypole dancing has recently been reintroduced (Figs. 5.16 & 5.17).

Mr Chapman continued to arrange school trips and more specific educational visits became an aspect of school life including an exchange link with a Birmingham school in order to help both sets of pupils learn about their different lives.

October 10th 1988 *Today the fourth year children were taken to Osmotherley to meet up with the group from Birmingham at the YHA. We played drama games to try to get to know each other.*

March 23rd 1987 *Today the older juniors visited the Eden Camp Museum at Pickering. We were the first school party to tour this new museum and the children enjoyed it and found it stimulating.*

May 19th 1989 *The lower juniors visited a local farm at Scaling to do some map reading exercises.*

June 4th – 7th 1990 *The annual trip to Edinburgh took place over this period. The youth hostel had been refurbished making the stay much more pleasant.*

Fig. 5.16 Maypole dancing behind the Downe Arms, 1994.

Fig. 5.17 Maypole dancing 1996, from Mrs Shepherd's scrapbook.

July 20th 1990 *The annual outing this year was to Beamish. A lovely warm day, which seemed to be enjoyed by all.*

April 10th 1991 *Today I visited Clarke Hall to prepare the visit in June. It is always a wonderful experience to visit Clarke Hall.*

June 10th 1991 *Today we visited Clarke Hall. The preparations leading up to the visit have been exhaustive. We visited the hall in role as a group of servants and a group of auditors who were to make an audit of each room in order to help Priscilla prepare for her imminent return to Derbyshire. Once again a superb occasion, everyone was thrilled and exhausted.*

The visits to Clarke Hall, near Wakefield, had continued for several years (Figs. 5.18, 5.19 & 5.20).

April 11 – 15th 1994 *I took a group of Year 5&6 children to an outdoor education centre (Ned Nook) near Keighley in West Yorkshire. The experience was shared with Lythe School and involved walking, swimming and trips to museums, castles and other places of interest.*

March 12th 1996 *Today the juniors visited Jorvik and the Eden Camp Museum. It was touch and go whether the trip was on due to SNOW. The drive was "hairy" and the Eden Camp experience one of the coldest trips imaginable. The Jorvik group needed wellies in the centre of York – say no more.*

There were also visits to the school by those who had interesting stories to tell and who added to the children's awareness of the wider world.

> November 24th 1992 *This afternoon Rev P Birkett came to the school to tell the children about his exciting journey to the Arctic in a fishing vessel with Captain Jack Lanaman.*
>
> October 10th 1993 *This morning the school was pleased to welcome Mrs Keunash Jolly, a representative of the Sikh community to talk to the children. She spoke about the Sikh way of worship, celebration and a brief history of Sikhism.*
>
> December 9th 1993 *Today started with Mrs McCabe's sister, a converted Muslim now living in Malaysia, talking to the school about Islam and Malaya. She brought her two children and samples of food and other ethnic items.*

The children even took part in a fashion show and, just as in earlier years, the log book, on occasions, recorded international events.

> April 27th 1994 *The fashion show was held in the Village Hall. It was a lot of fun and a great success. (The first S. African election took place today.)*

Fig. 5.18 Whole school visit to Clarke Hall, July 1981.

Fig. 5.19 Staff and helpers in their Victorian costumes ready for Clarke Hall.
Left to right – Mrs Marjorie Franklin, Mrs Phylis Craig, Mrs Mary Findlay, Miss Beryl Mason, Mrs Connie Watson, three parent helpers, Mrs Iris Hutchinson.

Fig. 5.20 Mr and Mrs Beeforth showing the children how to make corn dollies at Clarke Hall, July 1981.

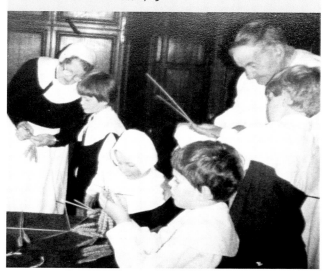

Although not a church school, Castleton School has always had close associations with the village church. As we have seen, the school was involved when the church of St Michael and St George was dedicated in 1926. Over the intervening years the children have made the journey up and down Castleton High Street for a number of services including Harvest Festival and, more recently, leavers' assembly. Ascension Day has often been celebrated with a service on the Howe. The children who play musical instruments have also taken part in Mothering Sunday and other church services. The local vicar and the Methodist minister both in their turn come into school to take assemblies.

> September 16th 1996 *Rev Lewis, the new vicar of Danby, called to introduce himself. His previous "parish" was Norway – a bit bigger than Danby.*
>
> May 8th 1997 *Joined with Danby School for an Ascension Day service on The Howe. The children played and sang and the heavens opened! A wet but enjoyable experience.*

There continued to be practical issues to deal with of course, including the weather (Figs. 5.21, 5.22 & 5.23). Inevitably the stove also gave trouble in spite of a new heating system being fitted in October 1992.

> October 5th 1988 *A power cut in the kitchen turned out to be the result of a mouse (now deceased) eating its way through a cable. Pest control were brought in.*
>
> February 8th 1991 *More snow – no bus children – the school is a swamp. A thoroughly messy end to the half term.*
>
> November 4th 1991 *School photographs were taken in the Village Hall – I have not seen it rain as consistently hard for a long time – I fear for the photographs as the children were a little damp to say the least.*
>
> October 26th 1992 *During this half term* (holiday) *the painters were in school making good the areas left by the heating contractors. Also Harrisons were in school building a permanent office in the library. On the Sunday of the holiday a carpet was fitted in the library.*
>
> January 19th 1993 *Mr Johnson the heating engineer called to check the boiler – he says it is not wired up correctly.*
>
> January 26th 1993 *This morning the boiler had not fired and despite three attempts to start it by hand the school remained cold. I contacted the maintenance office and they sent an engineer (10.30 a.m.). It seems the old storage tank is dirty and clogging the filter. I ordered more oil.*
>
> March 1st 1993 *Half term break ended with an Arctic spell of snow and high wind – as I write this the snow/hail is so loud I cannot hear the test match (India) on the radio.*
>
> September 13th 1993 *The weather continues to "dampen" the start to the year. The radiators remained cold – the engineer blamed the thermostat and the fact that, whilst very wet, the weather was not sufficiently cold to trigger the boiler.*
>
> October 14th 1993 *I contacted the heating engineer as the heating does not operate during the day. The engineer was not interested and his reply suggested he is as fed up as I am.*
>
> January 17th 1994 *The Year 6 children attended Eskdale School for drama and PE. I stayed at school to organise heating as the boiler had not fired in the morning.*
>
> November 17th 1995 *Today it snowed – the electricity failed and the children had to be sent home at 10 a.m. as the power had not been reconnected.*
>
> September 17th 1996 *An engineer called to look at our heating and use of energy as we use more than the average of energy/m². It is hoped to greatly reduce the cost of heating the school as a result of the survey.*

By 1997 there was a tradition at Castleton School of giving retiring staff a 'grand send off'. As Mr Chapman's term of office drew to a close he was certainly given a memorable leaving ceremony.

> March 20th 1997 *This was my final day with the children as tomorrow is a training day. The children gave me an unforgettable send off with an all singing and dancing event culminating in my feet in a bowl of warm water*

Fig. 5.21 Sometimes it rained. Children looking down on the Esk in flood.

Fig. 5.22 Sometimes it snowed.

Fig. 5.23 And one child even came to school on skis.

and spaghetti – custard pies and cold spaghetti on my head. This evening the parents and old friends and pupils arranged an evening in the village hall, once again songs and speeches but this time no spaghetti.

Unfortunately, the newly appointed head teacher was not able to take up his post until the following September. In the meantime it was left to an acting head, Mr Steve Clothier, to see the school through its first Ofsted inspection. Although only with the school for one term, Mr Clothier too enjoyed his time here.

July 23rd 1997 During the last 70 days I have developed a great affection for the school. I have been made very welcome by all and have re-discovered teaching skills from the distant past. I shall miss the school greatly and wish Adrian and his staff all the best for the coming years.

Mr Adrian Brixey arrived in September 1997 and before long had to deal with the issue of the stove, now referred to as a boiler.

November 12th 1997 *Heating engineer visited to try to sort out the boiler which has been running in an erratic manner.*

However, there was soon to be a particular highlight.

May 14th 1998 *Visit by His Royal Highness the Prince of Wales to Castleton Station. The school went to meet him, he talked to many of them. Mr Brixey then attended lunch at Danby Village Hall with other representatives of the area and Prince Charles. A very enjoyable day!*

Mr Brixey stayed at the school for two and a half years, seeing in the new millennium.

Pictures from the Archives

Mr Chapman giving a science demonstration.

School in snow, late 1980s.

School photo taken in the main classroom *circa* 1985.

The school, March 1987.

School photo *circa* 1992.

Visiting Botton 1993.

Easter Bonnet parade.

Finding out, late 1990s.

A scene from *Bugsy Malone*, December 1995.

Motor car from *Bugsy Malone*, December 1995.

Recorder group, 1996.

Back playground *circa* 1990.

Back playground 2014.

Four generations of Medds. In total five generations of this family have attended Castleton School.

Three Medd girls.

Rachel, Anna and Jack Chapman, the fifth generation of the Medd family to attend Castleton School.

Two Castleton School girls, the third generation of the Flintoft family to attend the school, look for Grandma's name in the log book for the 1950s - 1980s.

The New Millennium

ONE OF THE SCHOOL'S PROJECTS to celebrate the new millennium was to create a History Trail for Castleton. Mrs Young was acting head when it was launched.

June 23rd 2000 *An excellent presentation by the KS2 pupils who launched the History Trail. Mrs Shepherd is to be congratulated on her enthusiasm and perseverance in guiding the project. Members of the community who helped with the preparation of the guide were thanked and presented with gifts by the children. The launch was well attended by parents, governors and friends of the school.* (Figs. 6.1, 6.2 & 6.3)

The history trail continued to be sold locally over a number of years and raised hundreds of pounds for School Fund.

I came to the school in September 2000. In view of the recent changes, including two terms with acting heads, I was the fifth head teacher of the school in five years. This amount of 'turbulence' had caused some difficulties so there was plenty of work to do. However, I discovered that I had a wonderful team with me and we all worked well together, a very important factor in a small school (Fig. 6.4).

Keeping up the Castleton School tradition, I hadn't been long at the school before the heating system needed attention. One morning, just as the weather was turning colder, Mr McCulley, the caretaker, just

Fig. 6.1 The history trail in the making; children looking at their work in progress.

Fig. 6.2 Item No. 12 from the History Trail by Joe and Francis Cookson about Bow Bridge.

Bow Bridge **12**

Below the castle, crossing the fast flowing River Esk, was a Pack Horse bridge. This bridge was of the same date as the castle, and was built around 1175/85. It was called Bow Bridge. Peter Hudson of Danby, in his will of 1497 left 2 shillings for the repair of the "pons de Eske".

As this was one of few crossings of the fast flowing and dangerous River Esk between Commondale and Danby, this made the trading route between Cleveland to the north and the vale of Pickering to the south, easily defensible from the castle.

County Bridge

A new county bridge, built in 1860, is at a point just downstream from Bow Bridge. Both bridges stood side by side for thirteen years.
The old bridge was demolished in 1873, after a poorly attended local council meeting decided its fate.
Some of the stone from the old bridge was used in the building of the County School at Castleton in 1873/75.

By Joe & Francis Cookson

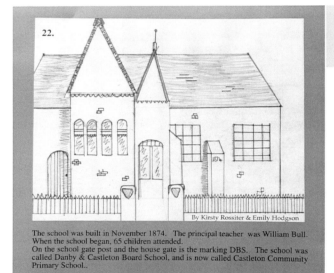

The school was built in November 1874. The principal teacher was William Bull. When the school began, 65 children attended.
On the school gate post and the house gate is the marking DBS. The school was called Danby & Castleton Board School, and is now called Castleton Community Primary School..

Fig. 6.3 Item No. 22 from the History Trail by Kirsty Rossiter and Emily Hodgson about Castleton School.

Fig. 6.4 Mrs Pam Shepherd and Mrs Christine Windwood planning lessons together.

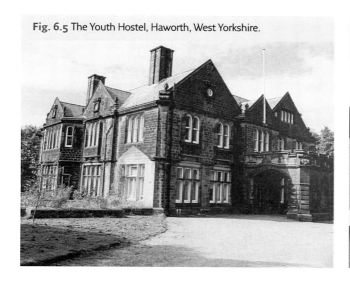

Fig. 6.5 The Youth Hostel, Haworth, West Yorkshire.

Fig. 6.6 Stuart Horton and Richard Thompson, beds already made at Haworth Youth Hostel, 2003.

could not get the stove to light and we had to close the school as the temperature was below the legal minimum for working. At least gone were the days when children (and staff) had to continue in sub-zero temperatures!

Like many of the head teachers before me I was keen to widen the children's horizons, to introduce them to a big, wide and wonderful world and especially for them to be aware of the multi-cultural nature of our society today.

> May 21 – 23rd 2002 *Yrs 5&6 trip to Malham Field Centre. 14 children and 4 adults went to Malham for three days to do a river study of Clapham Beck, visit Ingleborough Cave and walk from Tarn House to Malham. We also visited Gordale Scar. It was tough going at times as the weather was wet but the children didn't make one word of complaint and they worked hard. A very successful expedition.*
>
> June 24th 2002 *This morning Yrs R – 3 went to Whitby to go on board the replica vessel HM Bark Endeavour which came into port on Friday.*
>
> June 24 – 26th 2003 *Yrs 5&6 residential trip to Bradford staying at Haworth Youth Hostel. Visited the Cathedral, a Sikh Gurdwarah, had an Indian meal, shopped in Bombay Stores, attended a light and colour workshop at the photographic museum and saw the IMAX film Space Station.*

We made the Haworth/Bradford visit twice more during my headship and developed a particularly close relationship with the staff of the Cathedral and the Gurdwarah (Figs. 6.5 & 6.6).

2002 was the year of the Queen's Golden Jubilee. The whole school took part in a celebration to mark the event.

> May 30th 2002 *The children came to school today dressed in red, white and blue and we made rosettes, flags and coronets. At the end of the day the Rev Lewis came to school to present all of the children with a booklet and they also received a Yorkshire Post commemorative newspaper and a jubilee coin. (Figs. 6.7 & 6.8)*

A school photograph was also taken to mark the occasion (Fig. 6.9).

Sports and games were now a regular feature of school life and some particular events just had to be recorded in the log book.

> June 13th 2002 *Castleton 15, Danby 9 at the friendly netball match at Danby this afternoon. It is the first time in living memory that we have beaten Danby.*
>
> July 3rd 2002 *After lunch I took some of the Yrs 5&6 children to Stakesby School to the inter-schools athletics. Glorious afternoon – we came first in the throw.*

Fig. 6.7 Castleton School children celebrating the Queen's Golden Jubilee, May 30th 2002.

Fig. 6.8 The whole school, May 30th 2002. On the left Mrs Kath Dowson, centre left to right – Mrs Vilna Millns, Mrs Anne King, Mrs Pam Shepherd.

Fig. 6.9 School photograph, 2002. Adults left: Mrs Della Wedgwood, Miss Jodie Hughes, Mr Ian Hudson. Adults right Mrs Vilna Millns, Mrs Kath Dowson.
Back row: John Muir, Beth Havelock, Alice Hughes, Thomas Stanley, Philip Cook, Gary Helm, Freddie Taylor, Alex Boyd, Francis Cookson.
Second row: Joshua Helm, Matthew Williams, Joe Matthews, Joshua Blackburn, Robert Knowles, Sam Bye, Chloe Wilson, Catherine Sanderson, Jack Hepburn, Aaron Watson.
Third row: Briony Dodds, Donna Helm, Matthew Ayton, Tom Griffiths, Alana Wright, Sophie Playle-Watson, Bethany Watson, Tom Brooks, Sarah Keogh, John Liddle.
Front row: Joshua Mahood, Jimmy Matthews, Liam Watson, Ellie Wright, Mrs Pam Shepherd, Mrs Carol Wilson, Mrs Anne King, Michael Underwood, Hayley Booth, William Smith, Harriet Taylor.
Seated front: Victoria Nelson, Lily Day.

July 8th 2002 Sports Day. Had a carousel of events with children in teams. All went very well, a fine afternoon and Whitby Gazette photographer there to record events.

A sponsored walk towards the end of the summer term had also become a regular event during Mr Chapman's headship and this too continued.

July 16th 2002 School sponsored walk – the youngest children walked over the fields to Danby Church and back along the gated road while the older ones walked to Botton and back via Stormy Hall. Picnic lunches were taken on ahead in vehicles but we all carried water and wore hats. A very hot day. After school Mrs Shepherd and I took the netball team to East Whitby for a friendly match, which we drew 4 all.

Other fund-raising activities had been a regular feature of school life for some considerable time and we were all keen that these should carry on. We regularly joined in the Jeans for Genes appeal and in 2005 the school took part in the Big Hush.

January 28th 2005 Sponsored hush for the Macmillan charity. It was surprising how many children could be quiet for an hour! (Fig. 6.10)

One fund-raising activity that seemed to gain a momentum of its own was the Yellow Woods Challenge. This was the recycling of the Yellow Pages when they were replaced at the beginning of each year. The children took this on with gusto and even developed a friendly rivalry over who could bring in the most. In the end we had to beg storage space at Champion's garage for all the telephone directories. Over a number of years this enthusiasm raised in total well over £1000 for school funds (Fig. 6.11).

By the time I arrived at the school, Mrs Shepherd had been teaching after-school music for several years; over a period of time other activities were now added. We applied to the Ainthorpe Educational Trust for funding for some of these. The Trust gave us money towards a number of items including a telescope, which was used for our Sky High Club.

January 24th 2002 We have had two successful Sky High Club meetings this term so far. The first was cloudy weather so we looked at slides of the moon. The second was clear (but bitterly cold). We spent just half an hour outside but during that time we were able to see good views of the moon's craters, Saturn and its rings and Jupiter with three of its moons. Some of the children are becoming very knowledgeable about the night sky. March 19th 2002 Last Sky High Club for this season. Mr Lake talked to the children about the science of the telescope.

Fig. 6.10 The Big Hush, a sponsored silence for Macmillan Cancer Support, 2005.

Fig. 6.11 Mrs Pam Shepherd and Mrs Carol Wilson receiving a cheque for £300 for the Yellow Woods Challenge, 2004.

Fig. 6.12
School photograph, 2003.
Back row left to right – John Liddle, Jonathan Hepburn, Catherine Sanderson, Ethan Hulme, Alex Boyd, Robert Knowles, Aaron Watson.
Fourth row left to right – Mrs Kath Dowson, Mrs Wright (cook), Mrs Vilna Millns, Bethany Watson, Sophie Playle-Watson, Matthew Williams, Chloe Wilson, Joe Matthews, Sarah Keogh, Tom Brooks, Mrs Iris Hutchinson, Mrs Della Wedgwood.
Third row left to right – Jimmy Matthews, Joshua Mahood, Matthew Ayton, Sophie Rickelton, Alana Wright, Harriet Taylor, Briony Dodds.
Seated left to right – Robert Stanley, Peter Taylor, Lily Day, Mrs Pam Shepherd, Mrs Carol Wilson, Mrs Anne King, Victoria Nelson, Liam Watson, Taram Apia.
Front row left to right - Rowan Wilson, Rachel Muir, Ellie Wright, Hayley Booth, Finn Mahood, Rachel Chapman.

And one particularly magical evening:

February 15th 2006 *Sky High Club here this evening. Clear evening so we were able to see the Plough, Orion, Cassiopeia; watched the Seven Sisters rise above the school building.*

Botany club started in 2002.

June 25th 2002 *Botany Club after school today. Went out onto the moor – found star sedge, soft rush, milkwort and round leaved sundew.*

The last time it was entered in the log book that the school children had found sundew was 1910.

During the summer holiday of 2002 several refurbishments were carried out and a new school uniform was introduced.

September 9th 2002 *Term got off to a good start today and in smart classrooms too. The mobile classroom has been completely refurbished with new oil-fired radiators, a new floor and carpet and redecoration. The seniors' classroom has new curtains and the old sink unit has been removed. The children also look smart in their royal blue fleeces and sweatshirts.* (Fig. 6.12)

World Book Day had been a part of the school year for some time. In 2001 the children and staff dressed up as characters from their favourite stories (Figs. 6.13 & 6.14). Other days had different themes.

Fig. 6.13 World Book Day, spring 2001. Adults on the left – Mrs Christine Windwood as a pirate, Mrs Pam Shepherd as Tweedle Dum; on the right Mrs Christine Garforth as Tweedle Dee, Mrs Carol Wilson as (not so little) Little Red Riding Hood.

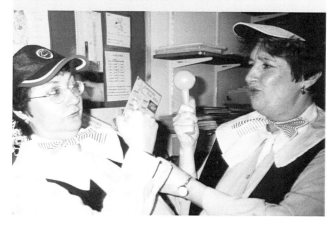

Fig. 6.14 Mrs Pam Shepherd and Mrs Christine Garforth as Tweedle Dum and Tweedle Dee, March 2001.

March 6th 2003 *World Book Day. Some of the children came to school in costumes from other countries, many brought in souvenirs from around the world. Each area of school was designated a different continent and their items exhibited for the day. During the morning the children created an international alphabet, learning about the original homes of animals, fruits and customs. Story session after lunch then open school.*

March 2nd 2006 *World Book Day. Collaborative workshop day. Most of the children brought in items from other countries to create a display for the day. In partnerships they then found out as much as they could about a country of their choice. All the children went on to make a postcard and to write a message from their country to a child at Rosedale Abbey School.*

One World Book Day was especially memorable.

March 1st 2007 *After lunch we all dressed up as characters from favourite stories. The children had some wonderful outfits, which ranged from Sleeping Beauty and a fireman to motor bike riders and Peter Pan. Mrs Shepherd looked splendid in a trench coat and trilby as Megadad from Eco Wolf, Mrs Gilbraith was Mrs Large from All in One Piece, Mrs Smith was Mrs Boot from Apple Tree Farm and Yours Truly was Fliss from the Merry Christmas Sleep Over in pyjamas and dressing gown complete with teddy bear and pigtails. The educational psychologist made an unscheduled visit this afternoon!*

Some of my favourite days during my time at Castleton School were those when we put all the children together and held collaborative projects. I am aware that some parents worry that the older and more able children will be 'held back' by such activities but in fact all of the research shows that both sets of children benefit, with the older and more able children benefiting most; they are able to consolidate their own learning while teaching someone else.

September 24th 2003 *While Mrs Shepherd was out with Y6, Mrs Mitchell and I had Yrs R – 5 together for a writing workshop. Each team produced a book on the history of Castleton School. The children all enjoyed looking at the school log books. I read to them the first entry of 1874 and my first entry in this book.*

October 15th 2003 *Whole school writing project to write a sequel to the KS1 children's story The Pink Princess. The children worked in teams, had to organise the workload and produced all text on the word processor.*

One particular collaborative book helped us to get through a difficult time at the school.

December 15th 2005 *School was informed this morning that we have a confirmed case of whooping cough and that children with bad coughs should be sent home and attend the surgery for a swab test. Only 15 children left at school and this evening's performance was postponed.*

December 16th 2005 *Fifteen children attended school today. We closed up the infant classroom and all worked in the main building.*

December 19th 2005 *Thirteen children attended school today. We all watched the DVD of How the Grinch Stole Christmas and then the children made their own book The Return of the Grinch recording what has happened to our Christmas and how we have "rescued" it.*

The previous year we had taken part in a very different collaborative project, joining with Lealholm School.

May 6th 2004 *Mrs Shepherd and I met with staff from Lealholm School to discuss the details of our Ammonite Adventure following our Royal Society award of £1900.*

June 11th 2004 *Lealholm's KS1 children visited us along with Chris Pellant, a local geologist.*

June 30th 2004 *The whole school went to Runswick Bay along with Lealholm School and local geologist Chris Pellant. We were joined by Luke Casey from ITV news and we all appeared on TV at the end of the day. A very successful fossil hunt in spite of the rain.*

This project continued for another full year, ending in July 2005.

But the ammonite adventure wasn't our only appearance on television. In March 2004 it had been Daffodil Day.

March 19th 2004 *Today it is 200 years since Wordsworth wrote his famous poem. We were visited by Francesca Garforth, a former chair of governors of the school who is also Wordsworth's great, great, great niece. The visit and the children's recitation of the poem were all caught on camera for ITV's news programme North East Tonight.*

There were many other enjoyable days – whatever the weather.

March 1st 2005 *Whole school walked up onto the Howe to build a snowman. Got caught in a heavy snow storm but all got safely back to school.*

October 20th 2005 *This afternoon Mrs Liddle came into school to talk about her role as a magistrate. The children then held a court – with me in the dock for not providing chocolate cake.*

October 21st 2005 *Brought the children chocolate cake for break time to carry out my punishment from yesterday.*

And the past was often part of the present.

March 20th 2006 *Mrs Connie Watson, former infants' teacher at this school, visited today to talk to the Key Stage 2 children about how the school has changed over the years. They took her on a tour of the school while she pointed out where the building had been altered e.g. where the Gothic door had been brought forward when the indoor toilets were fitted in the late '80s, the bracket where a gallery had once been in place above where the computer suite is now. Both she and the children enjoyed the visit.*

Christmas of course is always a special time in a primary school.

December 3ʳᵈ 2004 This afternoon the infants went down to Castleton Village Hall for our Christmas Craft afternoon with the playgroup children. A very glittery afternoon.

December 11ᵗʰ 2006 The whole school made Christmas cakes together this morning.

December 12ᵗʰ 2006 Children put marzipan on their cakes.

But there were serious issues too. One of the major developments in schools during my headship was the increased use of computers and access to the Internet. Immediately prior to my appointment a modem had been fitted and the school was finally online on 21ˢᵗ September 2000. The first purpose-built computer suite was fitted in 2005 and broadband arrived the following year. The school's website was launched in September 2006. Twenty-first century technology has given the children access to opportunities that were unthinkable just a short time ago.

June 8ᵗʰ 2004 Transit of Venus, KS2 looked at this on the Internet.

May 4ᵗʰ 2006 At two minutes and three seconds past one today it was 01, 02, 03, 04, 05, 06. This happens twice in the day, a.m. and p.m., but only once every 100 years. The whole school came together to watch this on the digital clock on the interactive whiteboard.

Mathematical problems, science experiments and historical re-enactments are just some areas of the curriculum that can be brought alive for the children through these technological developments.

The early years of the twenty-first century continued to see other changes in primary education. One was the introduction of several awards for schools. Castleton has gone on to gain several of these including the Healthy Schools and the Sportsmark Awards. The first was in 2004 – after several meetings and a great deal of paperwork.

June 23ʳᵈ 2004 This morning Mrs Shepherd and I were both observed teaching and the school was subsequently awarded the Primary Quality Mark.

September 24ᵗʰ 2004 A whole day of celebration for us. In the morning each school team created a poster depicting the school and these were taken to the village hall. In the afternoon we had our celebration assembly and the Primary Quality Mark award. The children were extremely well behaved and sang and recited well. They also enjoyed the strawberries and chocolate cake afterwards. The event was well attended by the community and visitors from the LEA, our former inspector and Mr and Mrs Dons (my former head) from Norfolk. (Fig. 6.15)

Fig. 6.15 Mrs Carol Wilson and Mrs Pam Shepherd with the Primary Quality Mark awarded to the school in 2004.

But the achievement I am particularly proud of is the development of the school garden. Built on a hillside, the school has always had a sloping playground. Even the first Ofsted report commented on this (but didn't suggest what might be done about it – jack it up perhaps?!). As already recounted here, the land adjacent to the school was bought in the 1980s. This was also part of the hillside so, inevitably, had a serious incline which, over the years, had slipped away and become steadily worse. In the health and safety

Fig. 6.16 *A humble but vernacular building.* The Tool Shed and Castleton Cottage, a new lease of life for the former outside toilets.

Fig. 6.17 The official opening of the newly terraced garden, October 2005. Mrs Delia Liddle, chair of governors, and Mrs Carol Wilson with Louis Playle-Watson, the youngest child, with the newly planted rowan tree, as tall as Louis at that time.

Fig. 6.17a The rowan tree in September 2014, now twice as tall as Louis who currently attends Eskdale School. Castleton's teddy continues to be taken home regularly by the children who help him to keep a diary of all his adventures.

conscious days of the twenty-first century, this vital asset had become more or less unusable but from the outset I had hoped that it might be terraced.

By 2005, the Local Management of Schools had enabled increased amounts of money to become available to individual schools. Some of this was known as Devolved Capital. As long as the LEA approved of proposed projects, Devolved Capital could be spent as governing bodies thought best for their school. North Yorkshire County Council was in agreement with the terracing of the Castleton School garden.

May 24ᵗʰ 2005 Simon Barker visited school this morning to look at the garden and quote for demolishing the outside toilets and terracing the garden. It has taken nearly five years to get this far but at last it looks as if we might have a proper, usable school garden.

In the event, we were not allowed to demolish the outside toilets. Being in the North York Moors National Park, we had to have planning permission for this. The Parks Authority found the former toilet block *a humble but vernacular building*. It had to stay, but it was also in the way. Fortunately, but with a great deal of difficulty, Mr Barker managed to get the digger up the bank from below in order to terrace the garden and the *humble but vernacular building* became a tool shed and a play house that was named Castleton Cottage (Fig. 6.16).

September 5ᵗʰ 2005 During the summer holidays Mr Simon Barker and his team have been working very hard in the school garden. The sloping site has now been terraced to create two 9m by 9m tiers and the potential for a third. The former outside toilet building has been converted into a tool shed and a playhouse and a gravel path laid from the new gateway behind the infant classroom and down the side of the garden between the terracing and the small copse of silver birch trees. It all looks very smart and we are proposing an official opening next month.
October 14ᵗʰ 2005 This afternoon we held our official garden opening. Fiona Campbell, from the LEA, came to plant a rowan tree and the vicar gave a blessing. We had about 60 visitors in all. Three musicians played Country Garden and all the children sang the Food Aid song. Tea was served indoors. (Figs. 6.17 & 6.17a)

Fig. 6.18 Mrs Carol Wilson and Mrs Pam Shepherd with the whole school on the new play equipment. Photograph taken to celebrate the Healthy School Award, June 2006.

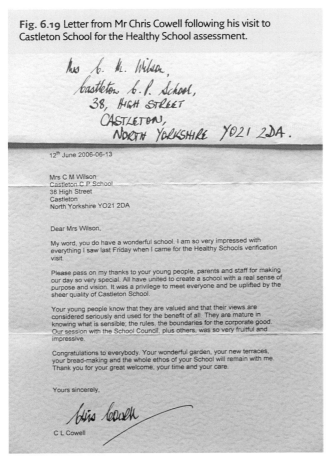

Fig. 6.19 Letter from Mr Chris Cowell following his visit to Castleton School for the Healthy School assessment.

Mrs C M Wilson,
Castleton C P School,
38, High Street
Castleton,
North Yorkshire YO21 2DA.

12th June 2006-06-13

Mrs C M Wilson
Castleton C P School
38 High Street
Castleton
North Yorkshire YO21 2DA

Dear Mrs Wilson,

My word, you do have a wonderful school. I am so very impressed with everything I saw last Friday when I came for the Healthy Schools verification visit.

Please pass on my thanks to your young people, parents and staff for making our day so very special. All have united to create a school with a real sense of purpose and vision. It was a privilege to meet everyone and be uplifted by the sheer quality of Castleton School.

Your young people know that they are valued and that their views are considered seriously and used for the benefit of all. They are mature in knowing what is sensible; the rules, the boundaries for the corporate good. Our session with the School Council, plus others, was so very fruitful and impressive.

Congratulations to everybody. Your wonderful garden, your new terraces, your bread-making and the whole ethos of your School will remain with me. Thank you for your great welcome, your time and your care.

Yours sincerely,

C L Cowell

For the first time since 1874, the children at Castleton School had a level playing field. Well, it wasn't quite a playing field but at least it was level. It was also a surprise to find that there was still considerable land remaining so the following year the third terrace was developed, covered in artificial turf and climbing equipment was installed (Fig. 6.18). And there was still some space left for growing vegetables.

It was wonderful to have so much extra play area. The younger children enjoyed Castleton Cottage and all of them appreciated the climbing equipment, which continues to be enjoyed today.

Mr Chris Cowell was the assessor for the Healthy School award. He spent the morning in school and subsequently sent me a personal letter as he had so much enjoyed his time at the school (Fig. 6.19).

Once again, there were to be staff changes. The school secretary is always a crucial member of the school team. Mrs Vilna Mills had been Commanding Officer in the secretary's chair for twenty years when she retired in December 2006. She was succeeded by Mrs Lucy Barker (Figs. 6.20 & 6.21). And there were other developments afoot.

The changing demographics that were affecting rural schools across the country were being felt at Castleton. In September 2005 we opened the school with just 28 children. While this was the lowest number on roll and numbers did rise again, this matter was giving concern to governors. It was also becoming increasingly difficult to recruit heads of small rural primary schools and the Local Education Authority was advising looking at other options in order to keep as many rural schools open as possible. By 2006, I was beginning to consider early retirement. Behind the scenes there began some low key discussions about federation and confederation, their relative merits and disadvantages.

As has already been recounted, we had some associations with Lealholm School and had begun to forge a closer relationship with Rosedale Abbey. We began to consider the possibility of confederation with the

Fig. 6.20 Mrs Vilna Millns retired in December 2006 after 20 years at the school.

Fig. 6.21 Mrs Lucy Barker came to the school as secretary in January 2007.

Fig. 6.22 Photograph in the *Whitby Gazette* following our successful Ofsted inspection, June 2007.

Great Ofsted!

Castleton School celebrates a good Ofsted report. Head Teacher Carol Wilson is pictured with pupils Gaby Ward, Ellie Wright, Rachel Chapman, Peter Taylor, Rachal Muir, Charlotte Knowles, Louis Payle-Watson, Michael Snaith   w 072419

latter. In the event, it was decided that the distance and high moorland between the two schools precluded this. As expected, when I did tender my resignation, the advertisement for a new head teacher drew few applicants but in March 2007 Mrs Jane Douglass was appointed to take up her post the following September. The governors breathed a collective sigh of relief.

March 23rd 2007 *Mrs Jane Douglass has been appointed head teacher from 1st September 2007. It was a unanimous decision and everyone is delighted.*

In the meantime, my last term saw the school's third inspection. The second one had been in September 2001 when the teaching was judged to be consistently good and the school had just four minor issues to attend to. Meanwhile, the inspection framework had changed, we were given much shorter notice and the inspection lasted a shorter time but seemed to be more intense. Everyone's hard work was duly recognised, however, and we came out with a report of a good school with outstanding features and the local press gave us suitable coverage (Fig. 6.22).

The weeks flew by and my last one at the school seemed to turn into one long celebration. I was showered with farewell gifts, some of them kept closely guarded secrets – but, thankfully, no spaghetti! (Figs. 6.23 – 6.26)

Mrs Douglass took up her position as the fifteenth permanent-post head teacher at Castleton School, in September 2007. Sure enough, she had hardly got her feet under the office desk when *the stove* needed attention.

Fig. 6.23 Presentation at farewell service Castleton Church, July 2007.

From Mrs Wilson's scrapbook.

Fig. 6.24 Wall hanging showing the hand of every child at the school, depicting all of the activities we had taken part in from 2000 – 2007. This was completed in secrecy with helpers even hiding under tables so that I didn't find out. It now has pride of place on my dining room wall.

Fig. 6.25 Mrs Wilson with all of the children on her last day at Castleton School, July 2007.

Fig. 6.26 Staff and governors at Mrs Wilson's farewell party at Westerdale Village Hall, July 2007.
Back row – Mrs Liz Smith, Mrs Lucy Barker, Mrs Pam Shepherd, Mrs Bev Mahood, Mr Ian McCulley.
Front row – Mrs Louise Smith, Mrs Hilary Thompson, Mrs Chris Gilbraith, Mrs Jane Dingle, Mrs Carol Wilson, Miss Karen Rees, Mrs Della Wedgwood.

Fig. 6.27 The Samba Band at Castleton Show, September 2008.

September 14th 2007 *We continue to have problems with our boiler pump. We have a new boiler, but the pump won't turn off. Ian* (Mr McCulley, the caretaker) *is trying to sort out who will accept responsibility.*

January 8th 2008 *We are having problems with our heating.*

But while the heating was giving its usual trouble, a great deal was going on. Music was clearly going to continue to be a signature feature of school life. Mrs Douglass soon began to seek extra funding for the school. Along with the recorder group, a samba band was now added to the school's activities.

February 4th 2008 *We have been allocated £960 to start a Danby/Castleton Samba Band. This is great news and could be the start of a whole Esk Valley project.*

April 18th 2008 *Our first Samba Club after school. Carolyn Champion came with some Danby children.*

April 25th 2008 *Our children performed their first outdoor Samba march for parents, led by Richard Brown, outside school this p.m.*

The school was soon gaining a reputation for its Samba Band.

September 12th 2008 *Samba Fantastic! What a brilliant day – we had several practices, including our after school club with Danby. We are ready for the show – we hope! Just shows what 3 teachers with a little musical experience between them can do (Actually we have a fair amount of experience, especially Pam and Carolyn – but we were well out of our depth with Samba!)*

September 13th 2008 *A really lovely day. The Samba band performed including lots of staff (nerve wracking!)*

Castleton School children have entered the village show for many years but this was a completely new venture and created a great atmosphere (Fig. 6.27). Even the Harvest Festival took on a new swing with the Samba beat.

October 8th 2008 *Harvest Festival in Castleton Church. This was a real fun event with the Samba Band marching into church and the children performing The Little Red Hen and The Flying Pizza.*

But there was more excitement to come.

October 10th 2008 *Dean Harris, our newly discovered Samba expert, came to take the first after school club today. Carolyn and I feel very excited about it and plan to enter the Eskdale Festival.*

The Festival was founded as the Eskdale Tournament of Song in 1902. As already recounted, the school had won prizes at the Tournament in the 1930s but it had been many years since there had been an entry from Castleton. Early in the following year, the children started to prepare for the Festival.

February 23rd 2009 *Today we had the first Eskdale Festival Samba practice at Danby. Oh dear! A long way to go.*

Fig. 6.28 In remembrance of Lucy Barker.

Mrs Douglass needn't have worried. The children rose to the occasion.

March 9th 2009 *Final Eskdale Festival preparation. Much better!*
March 10th 2009 *Eskdale Festival 8 p.m. performance. Wow! The Samba Band really made everyone sit up. What wonderful feedback we got and the parents and children loved it. Wonderful!*

Castleton's Samba band has gone on from strength to strength.

Unhappy news, of course, is not just the preserve of earlier centuries. It fell to Mrs Douglass to record a particularly sad event. Lucy Barker, the school secretary, had been absent from her post for some time.

March 3rd 2008 *Lucy is very ill. I was going to see her today but she is too poorly to see anyone.*
March 8th 2008 *Terrible news. Lucy died today. We knew she was ill but didn't realise how close to the end she was. What a tragedy.* (This was a Saturday.)
March 10th 2008 *Today has been so hard for everyone. Pam Shepherd and Jane Smithson, both of whom have had cancer and recovered, were in assembly. The staff cried openly and the children were shocked. I didn't think I would ever have to do anything like this. At about 11 a.m. Simon Barker called in to thank us for all we had done to support Lucy. We all feel a huge sense of loss and grief and of course feel so sad for Lucy's family.*

Lucy's funeral was held on 17th March in a packed Danby Church. Mrs Douglass recorded that she was given a *wonderful send off. What a wonderful lady she was.*

Later an item of furniture for the school grounds was bought as a memorial and was dedicated to Lucy Barker (Fig. 6.28). Lucy brought much joy to the school; she carried out her job with considerable flair and dedication and is greatly missed.

Fortunately, there were soon much happier events to record. Later that same year, Mrs Douglass was to oversee further developments to the fabric of the school. This was the first major building work to be undertaken since the office and staff room were installed in 1992 and the most radical change to the main school building since 1874.

June 23rd 2008 *Steve Wales from Jacobs came to look at our roof space with a view to a building project. We are all very excited. It seems very positive and hopeful we will be able to extend the building use in this way next summer.*
September 23rd 2008 *Steve Wales from Jacobs came to present the building plan to Nick Hood* (governor), *Delia Liddle* (chair of governors) *and me today. It's all very exciting, within budget, and can go ahead next summer.*
May 5th 2009 *Steve Wales came to discuss the building plans. It's all going well – on target to start as planned.*

Inevitably with such a large project, it wasn't always straight forward.

September 3rd and 4th 2009 *What a mad couple of days! We had extra staff in to try and get the building ready for the children after the roof project (which will be at least another couple of weeks). Wayne is busy decorating the dining room so it can be our junior classroom when the builders have finished. Nobody dare walk through!*
September 15th 2009 *Almost at the end of building and Sinclairs appear to have gone into administration. West Cliff Primary is left with half a roof. We think we've been lucky to get this far.*

It did take a little more time but eventually the job was finished. This imaginative use of the roof space has provided much greater floor area for the school in a way that was otherwise impossible within a listed

Fig. 6.29 In the pink. The opening of the computer suite coincided with Pink Friday. The children sang and played for visitors.

Fig. 6.30 Computers line the room in the roof space where the original beams are now shown to advantage.

Fig. 6.31 The new mezzanine floor is used as a library, music room and for assemblies as well as a computer suite.

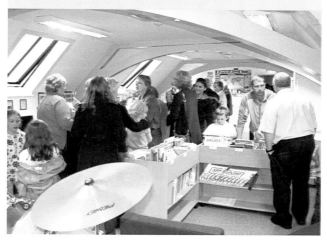

building. With a gift of a computer from the Salvation Army and £1000 raised by the PTFA, the computer suite/library/music room on the mezzanine floor could be put to creative use and it was given a grand official opening.

October 8th 2010 *At 3.00 p.m. was the opening of our computer suite. Introduced by the Samba Band marching in and playing. Delia Liddle cut the ribbon and made a speech. Keith Prytherch, head at the Community College, and Mark Taylor, head at Eskdale, attended with many community members.* (Figs. 6.29 – 6.31)

For her demonstration lesson at her interview for the headship post, Mrs Douglass had chosen to give a French class. This subject soon became well and truly embedded into the school curriculum and the children now *parlent un peu français*. The children were keen to share their new-found skills with parents and friends.

Fig. 6.32 *Bonjour tout le monde.*

Fig. 6.33 The children have learnt the days of the week in French.

February 6th 2009 *French afternoon – we performed songs, scenarios and a play for the community followed by French "snacks" in the village hall. A great success and some excellent accents!* (Figs. 6.32 & 6.33)

Other aspects of school life continued to be recorded in the school log book, including sports events and the weather.

December 4th 2008 *A snowy day! Most schools were closed but our staff and local pupils were here. What a lovely day! All our wellies were lined up in the foyer – it reminded me of a Gervase Phinn extract. We played games, built snowmen, had snowball fights and watched Snow Puppies DVD. Della* (Wedgwood) *and Gaby* (Boyd) *cooked dinner as Maria* (Gibson) *couldn't get here and we all ate together.*

January 16th 2009 *Wow! We won a football match against Oakridge. What a wonderful feeling. It's our first win. We now play in the Quarter Final of the Straws Cup … against Danby.*

February 12th 2009 *Dreadful weather. The snow fell very heavily so we sent home all the children who travel in. They were delighted of course!*

February 26th 2009 *A fabulous treat – birds of prey all morning. The owls were stunning and the hawks just wonderful. We all really enjoyed this experience.*

March 30th 2009 *We won a netball match! Our first win. Well done!*

July 1st 1009 *Our KS2 team won the small schools athletic shield.*

School visits continued to broaden the children's horizons.

June 2nd 2009 *Ten Y3 children from Breckon Hill Primary, Middlesbrough, came today with their teachers. They were delightful and fitted in so well. We are planning our return for July.*

July 9th 2009 *Our KS2 return trip to Breckon Hill. What an amazing experience. It made us realise how insular we can become. The school was full of many nationalities, mostly EFL* (English as a Foreign Language) *pupils. The head held a wonderful assembly speaking in French and leading into a French song, other English songs and poetry. Chris Gilbraith and I were touched by the lovely, responsive and well-behaved pupils. Our children were rather overwhelmed at being in a school of 300 pupils. They did very well, however, and enjoyed being with the Y3 class, although playtime was daunting.*

July 8th 2010 *Hindu Community Centre and Kirkleatham Museum visit. This was a very good school trip. The morning was stories of the Hindu gods told by the priest, followed by lunch in the community centre. Outdoor science at Kirkleatham in the afternoon was a perfect activity.*

In April 2011, once again the children enjoyed a right royal holiday to celebrate the wedding of the Duke and Duchess of Cambridge (Figs. 6.34 & 6.35).

Fig. 6.34 Castleton school children taking part in races at the street party for the wedding of the Duke and Duchess of Cambridge, April 2011.

Fig. 6.35 Castleton School children in procession for the Royal Wedding, April 2011.

Fig. 6.36 Mrs Pam Shepherd, Key Stage 2 teacher 1990 – 2009, nominated for Teacher of the Year.

There were changes to the staff as happens in any school. After nineteen years' faithful service, and working under no fewer than seven head teachers or acting heads at the school, Pam Shepherd took her marking pen from around her neck and left to make music elsewhere (Figs. 6.36). Hilary Thompson, who already knew the school, was appointed to teach Key Stage 2 from September 2009.

During the first two decades of the twenty-first century, the Ofsted framework had been changed several times. When the day arrived for the school to be inspected for a fourth time there was to be only one inspector and the period of notice was shorter than ever.

> November 23rd 2009 *Ofsted phone call! We are to be inspected Wednesday and Thursday this week.*
> November 25th 2009 *John Foster – one inspector only. We feel he already sees our school as "Good with outstanding features". Although this is a new Ofsted framework and supposedly harder to be Outstanding we need to prove that we have moved on from last time.*

November 26th 2009 Today our staff were amazing. We needed to show Outstanding teaching/subject leadership and progress from the last three years. Great team work from staff and Delia Liddle. We are now an Outstanding school. What a fantastic result for children, staff, governors, parents and community. Well deserved.

This was indeed well deserved and became the springboard for further developments. In January 2010, Mrs Douglass was asked to cover the maternity leave of the head of Fylingdales School. This was to be a foretaste of things to come and led to some interesting shared times.

March 31st 2010 Samba day at Fylingdales. All Castleton pupils went. The tutor was excellent. We ended the day with a Samba performance of 90 pupils. Wow!

While this shared headship between these two schools had a time frame, it sowed the seeds of the future as this sharing between the schools was found to be manageable and beneficial to the pupils. The school also took on a new role as a Leadership Development School, helping aspiring heads to gain a professional qualification.

In 2012, following the resignation of the head teacher at Glaisdale School, Mrs Douglass was asked once again to take on an acting headship. By this time, it had become even more difficult to recruit to headship and there were increasing financial constraints on small schools. Following detailed discussions between the governing bodies and parents at both schools, as well as the involvement of the LEA and the local community, a federation between Glaisdale and Castleton Primary Schools was formalised to begin in April 2013.

Both schools maintain their own budgets and buildings but share a head teacher and a governing body. This has enabled a pooling of resources, not least the all-important human resources of such small communities. Although the schools had been working together for some time, this agreement has now been enshrined in articles of federation, which has secured 'a robust and sustainable' future for both schools and enriched the teaching and learning for the children who attend.

No sooner had this arrangement got under way than Ofsted came calling again. Just two months into the formal federation, the school was to be inspected. In an ever-determined drive to raise standards, the bar for Outstanding had been raised once more so the spotlight was well and truly on both of these small rural primary schools and their federation. The resulting report was fulsome in its praise and Mrs Douglass and her team are to be heartily congratulated on such glowing commendation. Both schools and their federation were judged to be Outstanding.

Ofsted report for Castleton School June 2013 Pupils' achievement is outstanding. They typically have attainment which is well-above average and make outstanding progress from their starting points. Teaching is outstanding. Work is challenging and pitched at exactly the right level for all pupils. Marking is very well done so that pupils are clear about the level of their work and know how to improve it. Teachers make it extremely clear to pupils what they are to learn. They ask questions which stretch pupils. Teaching assistants are exceptionally skilful at supporting and teaching pupils of all abilities.

With the governing body, the head teacher has an extremely clear view of the school's strengths and relative weaknesses. They have skilfully managed the federation of two schools to the benefit of staff, pupils and the local community. This is clearly a school that continues to improve.

Castleton is now part of the Esk Valley Alliance, in association with the seven primary schools in the Upper Esk Valley. This collegiate way of working is a far cry from the isolation of earlier decades. All of the schools work closely together, sharing training and expertise as well as enabling the children to join with each other for a wide variety of lessons, musical events and sports fixtures. Castleton also has an integral role within a partnership of schools across Redcar and Cleveland as well as further afield in North Yorkshire.

Most recently the school has gone on to take a leading role in developments in education. It has become a National Support School, which means that the staff here are regularly asked to support other schools in challenging circumstances. Mrs Douglass tells me 'We are really proud to do this. We have developed relationships with colleagues in these schools which are lasting and which will enable us to learn from each other in the long term.'

The school has also become a National Teaching School, another considerable accolade. Castleton Primary School is one of eight such schools in North Yorkshire. Glaisdale and St Hedda's are two more, making three of the eight in the Upper Esk Valley. Mrs Douglass writes:

> This means that our school is able to be involved in leading change and development that has a real impact on education both now and in the future.

Mrs Thompson has become a Specialist Leader of Education, supporting trainee and newly qualified teachers, while Mrs Douglass is now a National Leader of Education.

And once again, changes are afoot for Castleton. As we go to press, Mrs Thomspon has just been appointed to her own headship at St Hedda's Primary School at Egton Bridge. We wish her well in her new post and, in the New Year, Castleton will look forward to welcoming a new Key Stage 2 teacher to join the team at this first class primary school.

Fig. 6.37 Castleton Community Primary School, autumn term 2014.

Pictures from the Archives

September 2000.

Enjoying painting.

Making biscuits in 2001.

Mrs Shepherd and recorder players in Castleton High Street, 2003.

The parachute is used for all sorts of co-operative games.

Mrs Linda Holmes helping children to sew.

A secret assignation after school, May 23rd 2003.

Looking for the source of the River Esk.

Mrs Shepherd has spotted it, 2005.

Visiting the drilling rig at Westerdale, January 2006.

Angelic host, 2006.

Farewell to Iris Hutchinson.

Summer Fair, 2007.

Sewing bag gift, July 2007.

Staff, July 2007.

Christmas production, 2012.

Maypole dancing.

Sports relief event, 2012.

Victorian Summer fair, 2014.

Former members of staff raise a glass to Castleton School. Vilna Millns, Pam Shepherd, Carol Wilson, Chris Galbraith and Jane Dingle.

$1 \times 2 =$

$2 \times 2 =$

$3 \times 2 =$

$4 \times 2 =$

$5 \times 2 =$

$6 \times 2 =$

$7 \times 2 =$

$8 \times 2 =$

$9 \times 2 =$

$10 \times 2 =$

Afterword

THIS YEAR Castleton Community Primary School is celebrating its 140th anniversary.

As Castleton Board School, it got off to an uncertain start in 1874. The managers of the school did little to encourage the pupils to attend and parents often kept their children working elsewhere. The first three head masters were far from qualified for the job, displaying a distinct lack of empathy for the learning difficulties of the children. Moreover, the school building was hardly fit for purpose.

Those early years were a period of isolation. There was little contact even with the neighbouring village school and head teachers had scant support from County Hall. Children were often unwell and some were unclean and infected with head lice. Some of them are likely to have suffered from malnutrition. In inclement weather they would arrive with wet clothes when they must have been bitterly cold in such a poorly heated school. Even the light levels were a cause for concern.

In the early years of the twentieth century, the long-serving head teachers Mr Groves and Mr Hay, in their respective terms of office, did a great deal to promote better attendance and to raise standards at the school. Subsequent heads have continued this trend and there have been considerable improvements to the building during the intervening years.

Castleton School has had a total of twenty-four head teachers, nine of whom were acting heads in post for short periods. The school has survived two world wars, countless models of stoves and boilers, seen periods of uncertainty and disappointment, taken part in royal events and national celebrations and gone on to win awards.

Today it is a warm, welcoming and safe environment highly conducive to teaching and learning. Children arrive in clean and tidy school uniform, have ready access to drinking water and enjoy a healthy school meal in the middle of the day. Their classrooms are bright, light and airy with state-of-the-art technology available to all. The playground is alive with stimulating opportunities for imaginative play while the garden enriches the curriculum as well as providing additional (level) play space for exploration.

There is no *creeping like a snail unwillingly to school.* The children tell me they like quiet reading time, mental maths and Bus Stop division. They like having extra friends within the federation and have recently found a duck's nest in the ivy in the garden. They like using their Tablets and 'looking up stuff. We don't get caned as in the old days or like in *Oliver Twist.* We love coming to school – especially home time and playtime!'

All of this because the school is guided by an active and well-informed governing body led by a head teacher of the highest calibre.

Castleton may still seem remote but its school is by no means isolated. Castleton Community Primary School is now a leader in the field of primary education. It has deep roots in the past, is an attractive and motivating learning environment of the present with its sights well and truly on the future. Long may that continue.

POST SCRIPT

As we go to press, I am reliably informed that after 140 years the stove is at long last behaving itself at school.

APPENDIX 1

HEAD TEACHERS AT CASTLETON SCHOOL 1874 – 2014

- November 1874 Mr William Bull
- December 1877 Mr Banks
- December 1879 Mr Thomas Gillibrand
- June 1888 Mr Walker
- June 1892 Mr Groves (29 years)
- September 1921 Mr Dale (temporary head)
- January 1922 Mr Jackson
- February 1926 Mr Charles Renton Hay (24 years)
- April 1950 Mr Ronald Reed
- September 1966 Miss Teresa Loo
- September 1977 Mr Stan Moore
- January 1982 Mr Dave Chapman
- September 1997 Mr Adrian Brixey
- September 2000 Mrs Carol Wilson (formerly Bennett)
- September 2007 Mrs Jane Douglass

There have also been several temporary head teachers at the school, usually owing to the head's illness:

- November 1879 Name unrecorded (for one month)
- September 1921 Mr Dale (for one term)
- January 1926 Miss Laurenson (for one month)
- June 1949 Miss Swift (for three month)
- September 1974 Mr Ross (acting head for three years)
- September 1981 Mr Nigel Snow (for one term)
- April 1997 Mr Steve Clothier (for one term)
- April 2000 Mrs Ros Young (for one term)
- December 2000 Mrs Christine Windwood (for six months)

APPENDIX 2

NUMBER ON ROLL

1874	65	in November	1919	58	(February)	1956	53		
1874	89	in December	1919	64	(June)	1958	53		
1875	103		1920	56		1959	54		
1881	89		1923	57		1960	49		
1893	89		1924	52	(January)	1961	62		
1897	104		1924	48	(July)	1962	63		
1896	87		1926	70		1963	62		
1898	105		1930	64		1966	61		
1900	105	(but average	1937	51		1969	65		
		attendance only 76)	1940	64		1970	58		
1901	89	(February)	1941	61		1983	58		
1901	103	(July)	1944	49		1985	50		
1902	96	(April)	1945	41		1987	57		
1902	102	(June)	1947	43		1988	63		
1902	105	(July)	1948	46	(April)	1989	59		
1903	99	(April)	1948	60	(June – after closure	1991	63		
1903	105	(July)			of Commondale	1992	65		
1903	98	(December)			School)	1993	69	(January)
1904	109	(July)	1949	47		1993	67	(September)
1905	98		1950	50		1994	78	(January)
1907	103	(May)	1951	58		2000	47		
1907	110	(November)	1952	59		2005	28		
1909	83		1953	58		2007	33		
1910	80		1954	60		2014	34		
1917	70		1955	55					

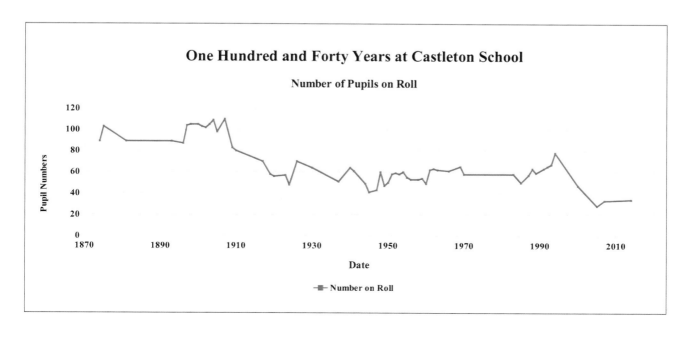

APPENDIX 3

STANDARDS OF EDUCATION FROM THE REVISED CODE OF REGULATIONS, 1872

STANDARD I

Reading One of the narrative texts in order after monosyllables in an elementary reading book used in the school

Writing Copy in manuscript character a line of print, and write from dictation a few common words

Arithmetic Simple addition and subtraction of numbers of not more than four figures, and the multiplication table to multiplication by six

STANDARD II

Reading A short paragraph from an elementary reading book

Writing A sentence from the same book, slowly read once, and then dictated in single words

Arithmetic The multiplication table, and any simple rule as far as short division (inclusive)

STANDARD III

Reading A short paragraph from a more advanced reading book

Writing A sentence from the same book, slowly read once, and then dictated in single words

Arithmetic Long division and compound rules (money)

STANDARD IV

Reading A few lines of poetry or prose, at the choice of the inspector

Writing A sentence slowly dictated once, by a few words at a time, from a reading book, such as is used in the first class of the school

Arithmetic Compound rules (common weights and measures)

STANDARD V

Reading A short ordinary paragraph in a newspaper, or other modern narrative

Writing Another short, ordinary paragraph in a newspaper, or other modern narrative, slowly dictated once by a few words at a time

Arithmetic Practice and bills of parcels

STANDARD VI

Reading To read with fluency and expression

Writing A short theme or letter, or an easy paraphrase

Arithmetic Proportion and fractions (vulgar and decimal)

PRIMARY SCHOOL CLASSES AFTER 1944

Following the 1944 Education Act the children were to be taught in primary and secondary schools. The primary school was divided into infants and juniors

Infants   Aged 5 – 7 years
Lower juniors   Aged 7 – 9 years
Upper juniors   Aged 9 – 11 years

From the mid-1980s some children started school in the year before they were five. They entered a Reception Class. This was subsequently known as Foundation Stage.

Following the Education Reform Act of 1988 the children in primary schools were divided into year groups in two key stages.

Key Stage 1   Aged 5 – 7 in two year groups:
Year 1   Children rising 6 years of age
Year 2   Children rising 7 years of age

Key Stage 2   Aged 7 – 11 in four year groups:
Year 3   Children rising 8 years of age
Year 4   Children rising 9 years of age
Year 5   Children rising 10 years of age
Year 6   Children rising 11 years of age

APPENDIX 4

MONEY, WEIGHTS AND MEASURES

12d = 1/-

20d = 1/8d

24d = 2/-

30d = 2/6d

36d = 3/-

40d – 3/4d

48d = 4/-

50d = 4/2d

60d = 5/-

70d = 5/10d

72d = 6/-

80d = 6/8d

84d = 7/-

90d = 7/6d

96d = 8/-

100d = 8/4d

108d = 9/-

110d = 9/2d

120d = 10/-

240d = £1

16 oz = 1lb

14 lbs = 1 st

2 st or 28 lb = 1 quarter

112 lbs = 1 hundredweight (cwt)

20 cwt = 1 ton

12 inches = 1 foot

3 feet = 1 yard

5½ yards = 1 rod, pole or perch

22 yards = 1 chain

10 chains = 1 furlong

8 furlongs = 1 mile

1,760 yards = one mile

4,840 square yards = 1 acre

2 gills = 1 pint

2 pints = 1 quart

4 quarts = 1 gallon

2 gallons = 1 peck

4 pecks = 1 bushel

APPENDIX 5

CHILDREN AT CASTLETON SCHOOL IN THE CENTENARY YEAR 1974

Kevin Williamson
Stewart Lillie
Gordon Booth
Robert Martin
Steven Thompson
Glenn Beveridge
Charles Balding
Adam Pacey
Christopher Smith
William Wells
Christopher Martin
Howard Watson

Robert Thompson
Russell Martin
Trudy Harding
Judith Sayers
Janice Hurst
Sally Watson
Christine Laws
Susan Jones
Jacqueline Grice
Sally Cook
Stephanie Smith
Elaine Gray

Peter Laws
Jeremy Williamson
Ian Westcough
Robin Cook
Craig Hitchinson
Owen Sayers
Anthony Booth
Iwan Koeller
Benjamin Randles
Andrew Cook
Jacqueline Medd
Julie Winspear

Joanne Chadwick
Claire Trousdale
Julie Kitching
Philippa Taylor
Melissa Pacey
Christine Jones
Louise Sainsby
Frances Whitton
Elizabeth Ann Martin
Anna Pearson
Maria Grout
Michelle Medd

David Findlay
Richard Findlay
Dougal Muir
Angus Muir
David Smith
Andrew Pinder
Simon Trees
Paul Muir
Adam Flynn
Michael Wildon
Barry Flintoft

Adam Hutchinson
Ian Kitching
Tracey Cook
Sarah Medd
Hayley Charter
Tina Hebron
Sophie Pacey
Jacqueline Simpson
Angela Grout
Elizabeth Randles

APPENDIX 6

CHILDREN AT THE SCHOOL AT THE 140TH ANNIVERSARY, NOVEMBER 2014

Daniel Hodgson

Ben Simpson

Evie Findlay

Holly Huggins

Maisie Todd

Jack Cook

Hazel Martin

Florence Day

Sadie Lancaster

Megan Needler

Max Robinson

Joshua O'Neill

Katie Harland

Isabel Hood

Honey Findlay

Samuel Wall

Archie Medcalf

Reuben Wall

Zoe Martin

Ella Richardson-Boal

Olivia Peacock

Oscar Taylor Forbes

Harry Thompson

Theo Bedingfield

Edie Medcalf

Hattie Walker

Emelia Towers

Josh Cook

Alfie Baker

Joseph Watson

Oscar Wall

JoJo Margetts

James Findlay

Seth Watson

APPENDIX 7

STAFF AND GOVERNORS OF CASTLETON COMMUNITY PRIMARY SCHOOL 2014

STAFF

Head Teacher	Mrs Jane Douglass
Teachers	Mrs Hilary Thompson (Teacher in charge)
	Mrs Caroline Barber (Part-time)
	Mrs Jill Leng (Part-time)
	Mrs Anne King (Part-time)
Classroom Assistants	Mrs Ruth Barrett
	Miss Heather Wilson
	Mrs Gaby Boyd (Relief)
	Mrs Kath Dowson (Relief)
Midday Supervisory Assistants	Mrs Kath Dowson
	Mrs Gaby Boyd
Breakfast Club	Mrs Kath Dowson
Secretary	Mrs Jean Blacklock
Caretaker/Cleaner	Mrs Karen Thompson
Cook	Mrs Gaby Boyd

GOVERNORS (CASTLETON & GLAISDALE FEDERATION JOINT GOVERNING BODY)

Our Governors play a vital role in our school life. Not only do they regularly meet as part of their role in the Leadership and Management of the school but they are also involved in many different aspects in the lives of the children whilst they are at school.

Mrs Delia Liddle	Chair
Mrs Jane Douglass	Head Teacher
Mrs Hilary Thompson	elected by the staff of the two schools (Castleton teacher)
Mrs Polly Findlay	Parent Governor, elected by Castleton parents
Mr Pascal Thivillon	Parent Governor, elected by Glaisdale parents
Mrs Denise Davidson	co-opted Governor
Mr Rob Hutt	co-opted Governor (Glaisdale Teacher)
Mrs Louise Margetts	co-opted Governor
Mr Peter Walker	co-opted Governor
Mrs Pam Groark	co-opted Governor
Mrs Susan Barlow	co-opted Governor
Mrs Penny Walker	co-opted Governor
Louise Davis	Clerk to the Governing Body

SCHOOL AIMS

- To create a warm, supportive and stimulating school environment in which children feel happy, safe and secure, and are eager to learn.
- To develop positive relationships founded on mutual trust, respect and good example.
- To ensure all pupils are encouraged and supported in reaching their potential as learners.
- To provide all children with a broad, balanced curriculum relevant to their needs and abilities.
- To develop children as caring, sensitive and tolerant individuals who have a clear understanding of right and wrong.
- To introduce children to a wide range of experiences and challenges which motivate and enrich their learning now and in the future.
- To have high expectations of all children in terms of learning and behaviour.
- To value all children equally, upholding their rights regardless of gender, ability, disability, colour or race.
- To promote a strong partnership with parents based on shared information and responsibility for children's learning.
- To promote links with the Esk Valley Alliance and other schools to enrich the experience we can offer our children.
- To serve the community well, encouraging and welcoming support, co-operation and interest, and inspiring confidence and pride in the work of the school.